The God Centered Marriage

Susan J Nelson

ISBN: 1720422346
ISBN-13: 978-1720422341

DEDICATION

I dedicate this book to my husband, Mike. You are the perfect example of a godly man and just about the most perfect (and most loved!) man to ever walk the earth. You make me believe that anything is possible . I look forward to our next adventures and can't wait to see where God leads us.

CONTENTS

ACKNOWLEDGMENTS

This book would not be possible without the love and support of my husband, Mike, my children, Brett and Hunter, my bonus children, Nicole and Christian and my mother-in-law, Linda. You continue to teach me new things and motivate me to be a better wife, mother and daughter. I love you all.

Introduction

Hello, Sweet Friend! I am thrilled that you have joined us to explore how to put God at the center of your marriage.

Let us begin with some insight from Genesis:

Genesis 2:18-24

18 The LORD God said, "It is not good for the man to be alone. I will make a helper suitable for him."

19 Now the LORD God had formed out of the ground all the wild animals and all the birds in the sky. He brought them to the man to see what he would name them; and whatever the man called each living creature, that was its name. 20 So the man gave names to all the livestock, the birds in the sky and all the wild animals.

But for Adam[a] no suitable helper was found. 21 So the LORD God caused the man to fall into a deep sleep; and while he was sleeping, he took one of the man's ribs[b] and then closed up the place with flesh. 22 Then the LORD God made a woman from the rib[c] he had taken out of the man, and he brought her to the man.

23 The man said,

"This is now bone of my bones

   and flesh of my flesh;

she shall be called 'woman,'

   for she was taken out of man."

24 That is why a man leaves his father and mother and is united to his wife, and they become one flesh.

Perhaps you have picked up this book because your marriage is hurting and you are desperately seeking help to restore what God has joined. On the other hand, maybe your marriage is good, but you are looking for practical ways to put God at the center of it. You might even fall somewhere in between. Regardless of what brought you here, I am grateful that you have joined this journey with us and I pray that the content will bless you, your husband and your marriage.

In this course, we will explore what it means to have a God centered marriage and learn practical steps you can take to place God firmly at the head of your union.

Each chapter includes:

- An exploration of an area of marriage that needs to have Jesus at the center
- Action Steps to take
- Prayers for your husband and your marriage
- Study Guide/Journaling prompts

What you will need in addition to this book:

- A Bible
- A journal or notebook
- Printer (optional)
- An open heart and mind

You can access additional resources and materials at:
https://womanofnoblecharacter.com/the-god-centered-marriage-book/

There you will find:

- Video lessons

- A printable poster

- Scripture memory cards

- Printable checklists

- Bonus material

Just a few notes on the content of this book. You do not HAVE to do all of the content and activities in order, however, I recommend that you complete as many as you can. The more you put into your commitment to putting God at the center of your marriage, the more you will get out of it and stronger your marriage will be.

I do recommend that you keep a journal throughout your reading of the book. Use it to record your prayers, your struggles and your victories along the way. If you aren't sure how to journal or what to journal about, use the study guide to help you. God WILL answer prayers and I am confident that as you put Him at the center of your marriage, your marriage will grow stronger and more intimate. Keeping a journal will help you see the progress you are making and how God is answering prayer.

Give yourself time to work through each chapter and the study guide, write in your journal, enjoy an activity and pray about that week's focus.

You can always go back and review previous sections.

One final note before we begin. For all scripture references, unless otherwise noted, I will be using the NIV for consistency. Feel free to look up the verses in the translation that you are most comfortable with.

Are you ready to have a God centered marriage?

God Created Man and Woman

In Genesis 2:18-24, we are given a glimpse into the beautiful moment that God created Adam and then Eve. We are also shown why: 18 The LORD God said, "It is not good for the man to be alone. I will make a helper suitable for him".

Let's look at the entire passage for a moment:

Genesis 2:18-24

18 The LORD God said, "It is not good for the man to be alone. I will make a helper suitable for him."

19 Now the LORD God had formed out of the ground all the wild animals and all the birds in the sky. He brought them to the man to see what he would name them; and whatever the man called each living creature, that was its name. 20 So the man gave names to all the livestock, the birds in the sky and all the wild animals.

But for Adam[a] no suitable helper was found. 21 So the LORD God caused the man to fall into a deep sleep; and while he was sleeping, he took one of the man's ribs[b] and then closed up the place with flesh. 22 Then the LORD God made a woman from the rib[c] he had taken out of the man, and he brought her to the man.

23 The man said,

"This is now bone of my bones

   and flesh of my flesh;

she shall be called 'woman,'

   for she was taken out of man."

24 That is why a man leaves his father and mother and is united to his wife, and they become one flesh.

4

God Created Male and Female

God created both man and woman in His own image, but they were created male and female. When our children are small, we teach them to identify a man and a woman. Daddy is a male and Mommy is a female. Brother is male and sister is female. Grandpa is male and Grandma is female. Of course, we are pointing out the physical differences between the two genders. Soon, children are able to easily identify people they encounter as male or female.

The differences between man and woman extend far beyond physical characteristics, though. Men and women view the world differently, they have different styles of communicating, different ways to deal with the stress and pressures of this world.

How we are created differently

Of course, not all men are the same as other men and not all women are the same as other women. We each have unique personality and character differences that make us who we are, but let's stay with the basic generalities of the differences between the sexes to help us better understand our husbands.

Men were created to:

- Hunt
- Provide
- Generate/produce
- Fight (as in a warrior)
- Achieve, succeed, win

Men, when meeting someone, tend to identify with their occupations. If asked to tell about themselves, they would likely respond with "I'm Mike. I'm a plumber and I like to golf". Ok, so I'm being very simplistic here, but I think you get the point.

Women, on the other hand, were created to:

- Nurture
- Gather
- Be peacemakers
- Relate
- Cultivate
- Connect

Women, when meeting someone and asked to tell about themselves, would likely respond with something like "I'm Sue, I'm married to the love of my life and mother of two great kids".   Do you see the difference here?

While many women have successful careers and work outside of the home, they were created to be nurturers and crave relationship with others. They identify mainly by those relationships.

Communication

Women also tend to be more verbal than men. Even as children, studies have shown, that girls have a larger vocabulary than boys. They are more likely to "use their words" than little boys. Boys, on the other hand, communicate more with sounds and actions. They use grunts, exclamations (pow, vroom etc.) and, even physical actions to communicate. Boys are more likely to throw a toy or strike another child when they are frustrated.

Women tend to share their feelings more. Men tend to share information more. Women tend toward communication, men toward action.

Sexuality

Many marriages struggle in this area due to the differences in how we were created. Men see sex primarily as a physical act. Women usually view sex as an emotional act.

For men, seekers of beauty, sexual attraction usually begins with what they see - a woman's body, her hair, her breasts (just being real here).

For women, however, while they may notice and appreciate a man's physical attributes, they are likely to find a man's non-physical characteristics attractive first– his laugh, his humor, his compassion.

Men and women respond to sexual attraction differently, as well. Men are more impulsive and reactive. It may be more difficult for them avoid temptation as they are wired to be aroused by physical sights and images (thus the reason that so many men struggle with pornography).

Women are more likely to become aroused by the words she hears and the attentiveness of her husband, even his gentle touch.

Of course, these are general differences and all may not entirely reflect you or your husband.

Think for a moment about you and your husband. Would you agree or disagree with these differences?

We could spend days parked here discussing the differences between how God created man and woman differently, but I just wanted to point out that we ARE created differently and that those differences can be little chips that cause a marriage to crack if not recognized and navigated with wisdom and grace.

I would be remiss, however, if I didn't point out that these differences are also designed to compliment each other. We'll talk about that more in future chapters.

Study Guide:

What evidence do we have that God established male headship at creation?

What is the significance of creating Adam first, and then Eve, instead of creating them as a pair as He did with the animals?

What is the significance of God bringing Eve to Adam so that he could name her?

Share some examples of how men and women were created differently:

In what ways do men and women communicate differently?

What problems can occur if we fail to recognize the differences between men and women and how they view the world?

Chapter 1

God's Design for marriage

Today we are diving into our study of the God Centered Marriage. We'll be taking a look at God's plan for marriage and how scripture commands that we love our spouses.

One of my favorite verses is from Ecclesiastes 4:12, it reads:

Though one may be overpowered,

two can defend themselves.

A cord of three strands is not quickly broken.

When God is at the center of our marriage, we are forming a three cord strand. Think of the strength of one strand, then two, then three. You are one strand, your husband the second and God, the third. Think of the strength you gain when your cord becomes a cord of three instead of one or two!

In Mark 10:9, we read "Therefore what God has joined together, let no one separate."

How wonderful is the comfort of knowing that with God at the center of your marriage, you are giving your marriage the strength to withstand everything that is thrown at it! He will be your refuge and strength in times of trouble!

Some of our discussion may be uncomfortable. God may convict you through His Word and shine a light on an area that you need to improve.

As I was writing this course, God convicted me. My husband and I have a wonderful marriage, but, as I was creating the course outline and listing all of the areas of marriage, specifically, how to put God at the center of it, He was whispering in my ear that maybe I'm not giving ALL of my marriage to Him.

I'll share more as we unpack each section, but I want you to take heart. Spirit work can be uncomfortable, but if you come to God and ask Him to take the lead in your marriage and your heart, He delights in that and you will be changed.

So let's jump in and look at God's standard for marriage, shall we?

Join me in the reading material section for Chapter 1 where we will examine the three things we need to do to put Christ at the center of our marriage.

God's Standard for Marriage

Throughout Scripture, we are taught the roles of husband and wife and how to live our lives according to His plan for these roles. In my Intro to Proverbs 31 course or and the membership program, Faith Filled Home, we deep dive into the role of wife. For men, there are numerous resources on the role of the husband, as well.

All are great to study and strive for, but for our purposes, let's focus solely on God's standard for marriage, as a whole.

In Ephesians we receive this command plainly.

Ephesians 5:25:

Husbands, love your wives, just as Christ loved the church and gave himself up for her

Ephesians 5:22

Wives, submit yourselves to your own husbands as you do to the Lord.

It seems pretty straightforward, doesn't it? Yet, many of us fail to live by these standards. When we look at God's steadfast love for us and hold that love up to compare it with the love we have for our husband's, where are we falling short?

To put God at the center of your marriage and follow His standard for your marriage, we need to do three main things:

1. Establish your priorities by the Lord and His Word.

God makes our priorities pretty clear. We are to love God first, then our husbands and everything else, yes EVERYTHING, including your children, follow.

The Lord desires that we love him more than we love anything else. The best way to develop a love for the Lord is to think about and examine (in Scripture) all the ways he has loved you. There are so many other things that could compete for our mental energy and emotional love. Women, especially, have a hard time with this one.

The Lord desires that we serve him. However, there are many couples who spend very little, if any time, serving the Lord. The vast majority of their time is dedicated to other things. If you are not actively using your gifts and abilities to serve the Lord, then Christ is not at the center.

God also desires for us that we are to be good stewards of the resources he has given us. So when couples use the financial resources to accomplish things for the cause of Christ, they are demonstrating the priority of the Lord in their life. Jesus said where your treasure is, there will your heart be also. It is impossible to have Jesus at the center and not invest financially in the work of the Lord.

There are dozens more examples, but the point is that our priority system will be measured largely by the way we invest our time, talent, and treasure.

2. You think about the Lord in the mundane moments of life.

Life is busy. We have errands, laundry, work, meetings, cooking; the list goes on and on. In the mundane moments of our lives is when God wants us to focus on Him. Are you including Him in your day? In your moments?

Recently, I shared in a blog post, how much I can't stand mopping floors. Seriously, I just dislike that chore. Instead of feeling resentful that I have to mop the floors AGAIN, I mean, didn't I JUST do this?, I've found that by thanking God for floors to mop and talking with Him while I mop that the chore doesn't seem so bad.

Think about God and praise Him in the little moments of everyday. Praise Him and talk to him while you are preparing your family's meals, when you are in the car or waiting for your little one at practice. Share with Him your frustrations and your joys.

If you and your husband are disagreeing, instead of stewing about it, consider "How does God want to use this argument and how I respond to it to help me grow to be more like Christ?" "What do I need to learn about my spouse?"

Use those moments as an opportunity for you to grow and change not an opportunity for you to blame your husband or build up resentment.

We have a tendency to pray when we need something or when something is going wrong in our lives, but if we include him in all of the moments in our days, we are putting Him first and therefore, putting Him at the center of our marriages.

3. You maintain spiritual disciplines.

What do you think of when you think of Spiritual disciplines? Spiritual disciplines can include prayer, Bible study, fasting and attending worship services, of course, but there can be more to it then the obvious. They are activities that help you live with Jesus as the center. Prayer is a conversation with the Lord. It doesn't have to be fancy or formal, in fact, since God wants your heart, He wants you, the real you. The way you naturally talk with a friend. He wants you to talk with Him like that. Do you enjoy talking with God? The more you talk with Him, the more you will enjoy it and the more you enjoy it, the more you will want to talk with him.

Establish a lifestyle of prayer.

While we are on the subject of prayer, don't just pray FOR your husband, pray WITH your husband. Prayer is an intimate act and praying together allows you to be vulnerable and opens the heart to deeper connection with your spouse.

Living a life with Christ at the center your life, of your marriage is pure joy.

Prayer:

Lord, please help me to love my husband the way you love us. Strengthen us each day and remind us to ask You into every nook and crevice of our relationship. Heavenly Father, please remind us daily that without you our cord is not fortified. We need you to be at the center of our marriage to help us withstand the trials that we face. Lord God, equip me to be the helpmeet that you have created me to be. Shield us from temptations that rearrange our priorities. Help us to love as you love us, with a steadfast love. In your Son's Holy name, I pray. Amen.

Action Plan:

Commit to praying FOR your husband every day. If you don't know where to begin, consider this free challenge on Praying for Your Husband by Woman of Noble Character

Commit to praying WITH your husband every evening

Consider doing a couple's devotional together. (My husband and I have done a nightly devotional for years. It has blessed our marriage immeasurably and has deepened not only our love, but helped put God at the head of our marriage) See Chapter 1 resources for suggestions.

Make prayer a part of your mundane moments of life. Talk with Him as you go about your day.

Although it may be uncomfortable, be sure to make your priorities reflect His will: God, Your Husband and then everything else.

Study Guide:

Consider your relationship with your spouse as a reflection of your relationship with Jesus. What there adjectives would you use to describe your marriage?

Are these the same adjectives you want to describe your relationship with Jesus? If not, what changes do you need to make?

Above, we read God's standard for marriage found in Ephesians 5:25 and 5:22

What are common excuses people give for not obeying these commands?

Are you guilty of using these excuses?

Read 2 Corinthians 14:16, 26 and 16:7

What three areas of your marriage most need the Holy Spirit's help?

Do you put God in all of the little moments of your day? If not, what can you do to include him in the big as well as mundane tasks of daily life?

Chapter 2

Building Strong Foundations & Learning to understand each other's needs

Is a God Centered Marriage becoming clearer to you now? I pray that it is.

Today, we are going to begin to lay the foundation of placing God at the head of your marriage.

When a builder builds a home, he doesn't just grab some wood and nails and start building. He draws up blueprints, makes his material list and buys what he needs. Then the ground is dug and concrete foundations are poured.

In chapter 1, we dug the ground and today, we are going to pour the concrete.

How do we build a strong foundation in our marriage? The first step is being firm in our own faith. In Matthew 10:37-39, we read:

37 "Anyone who loves their father or mother more than me is not worthy of me; anyone who loves their son or daughter more than me is not worthy of me. 38 Whoever does not take up their cross and follow me is not worthy of me. 39 Whoever finds their life will lose it, and whoever loses their life for my sake will find it.

Dear friend, we cannot have a God centered marriage if we, ourselves, do not put Christ first.

How is your faith? Is it unshakeable?

When we understand what God is teaching us in Matthew 37-39, we begin to understand the Great Commandment "Love the Lord your God with all your heart and with all your soul and with all your mind". Only then can we truly understand the next great commandment: "Love your neighbor as yourself".

When we put God first and understand love as God intended, we learn to love others in that same way.

In the Bible, this type of love is called "Agape". I love the definition of agape from Got Questions.org:

The Greek word agape is often translated "love" in the New Testament. How is "agape love" different from other types of love? The essence of agape love is goodwill, benevolence, and willful delight in the object of love. Unlike our English word love, agape is not used in the New Testament to refer to romantic or sexual love. Nor does it refer to close friendship or brotherly love, for which the Greek word philia (or phileo) is used. Agape love involves faithfulness, commitment, and an act of the will. It is distinguished from the other types of love by its lofty moral nature and strong character. Agape love is beautifully described in 1 Corinthians 13.

Let's take a look at 1 Corinthians 13 for a moment to paint a word picture of Agape love:

1 Corinthians 13

13 If I speak in the tongues[a] of men or of angels, but do not have love, I am only a resounding gong or a clanging cymbal. 2 If I have the gift of prophecy and can fathom all mysteries and all knowledge, and if I have a faith that can move mountains, but do not have love, I am nothing. 3 If I give all I possess to the poor and give over my body to hardship that I may boast,[b] but do not have love, I gain nothing.

4 Love is patient, love is kind. It does not envy, it does not boast, it is not proud. 5 It does not dishonor others, it is not self-seeking, it is not easily angered, it keeps no record of wrongs. 6 Love does

not delight in evil but rejoices with the truth. 7 It always protects, always trusts, always hopes, always perseveres.

8 Love never fails. But where there are prophecies, they will cease; where there are tongues, they will be stilled; where there is knowledge, it will pass away. 9 For we know in part and we prophesy in part, 10 but when completeness comes, what is in part disappears. 11 When I was a child, I talked like a child, I thought like a child, I reasoned like a child. When I became a man, I put the ways of childhood behind me. 12 For now we see only a reflection as in a mirror; then we shall see face to face. Now I know in part; then I shall know fully, even as I am fully known.

13 And now these three remain: faith, hope and love. But the greatest of these is love.

Agape love is a sacrificial love. It is denying self for the benefit of God or your beloved. It is love in action, not just words. It is reflecting the love that God has for us on others.

As you go through the material for Chapter 2, examine your relationship with our Heavenly Father. Read His Word to learn more about how He loves us. Then see how your love for Him and your husband measures up against that love.

In this chapter, we will also take a look at the Five Love Languages by Gary Chapman. If you've never read the book, I encourage you to pick up a copy. You can find it here or in your local bookstore.

Learning how your husband feels love is an important step in loving him the way God intended.

One quick note: This chapter's reading material and study guide are quite lengthy. I encourage you to spend some time each day, over the course of a week or more to dig into it and truthfully and prayerfully go through the study guide.

Are you ready to dive in? Let's go!

The Five Love Languages

The Five Love Languages: How to Express Heartfelt Commitment to Your Mate is a 1995 book by Gary Chapman. It outlines five ways to express and experience love that Chapman calls "love languages": gift giving, quality time, words of affirmation, acts of service (devotion), and physical touch. Examples are given from his counseling practice, as well as questions to help determine one's own love languages.

According to this theory, each person has one primary and one secondary love language.

Chapman suggests that to discover another person's love language, one must observe the way they express love to others, and analyze what they complain about most often and what they request from their significant other most often. He theorizes that people tend to naturally give love in the way that they prefer to receive love, and better communication between couples can be accomplished when one can demonstrate caring to the other person in the love language the recipient understands. An example would be if a husband's love language is acts of service, he may be confused when he does the laundry for his wife and she doesn't perceive that as an act of love, viewing it as simply performing household duties, because the love language she comprehends is words of affirmation (verbal affirmation that he loves her). She may try to use what she values, words of affirmation, to express her love to him, which he would not value as much as she does. If she understands his love language and mows the lawn for him, he perceives it in his love language as an act of expressing her love for him; likewise, if he tells her he loves her, she values that as an act of love.

I encourage you and your spouse to take the free online quiz to determine each of your love languages. Then, talk about it and see if you are surprised by any of the results.

When my husband Mike and I did this, we were really surprised by each of our results. Knowing how the other prefers to experience love has helped us to show that love in a way that has strengthened our marriage even more.

The 5 Love Languages® profile will give you a thorough analysis of your emotional communication preference. It will single out your primary love language, what it means, and how you can use it to connect with your loved one with intimacy and fulfillment.

Let's briefly look at each of the 5 Love Languages:

GIFTS

On the 5 love languages website, the description of Gifts shows this:

"Don't mistake this love language for materialism; the receiver of gifts thrives on the love, thoughtfulness, and effort behind the gift. If you speak this language, the perfect gift or gesture shows that you are known, you are cared for, and you are prized above whatever was sacrificed to bring the gift to you. A missed birthday, anniversary, or a hasty, thoughtless gift would be disastrous – so would the absence of everyday gestures. Gifts are visual representations of love and are treasured greatly."

Basically, it is not that someone with a love language of gifts is materialistic or only looking for expensive gifts. Instead, this person feels loved when their beloved picks up their favorite candy bar when at the store or buys them a book that reminded them of their loved one. They even love handmade or handwritten gifts. It is truly the though behind the gift – the knowledge that their loved one was thinking of them, that makes the gift so warmly received.

My husband has a love language of gifts and, if you met him, you might be surprised to learn that. He is not at all materialistic, but he loves receiving gifts from the heart.

I asked him to share with me some of the gifts that he has received from me that meant the most. Here's what he said:

• M&Ms personalized with his favorite baseball team

• A steering wheel cover branded with his favorite football team

• A story that I wrote for him about how we met and how our story evolved

• When I surprise him by picking up his favorite snack at the store

• A scavenger hunt that I created for him to find clues and mini gifts related to our love story

What's the overarching theme here? All of the gifts were free or relatively inexpensive, but they all took time and made him know that I was thinking of him and his happiness when I bought them or created them.

QUALITY TIME

Continuing with some of the Love Languages, many people feel love by quality time spent with their spouse. Quality time can vary from person to person but generally, "quality time" is defined as: time spent in giving another person one's undivided attention in order to strengthen a relationship.

What a couple actually does during their quality time varies and can be as unique as the couples themselves. For some, it is being engaged in an activity together (for example, playing a board game or mini golf). For others, it is just being together (going for a walk or watching a movie together).

What are some things you enjoy doing to have quality time with your spouse? List them below.

Now ask your spouse what things he enjoys doing with you to have some quality time. List them below.

With lives being so busy and family obligations taking up so much of our time, I often hear that couples just can't make time to be together and enjoy quality time. I say "hogwash'! You find time to cook dinner or shop for groceries. You find time to run errands or attend your nieces' soccer game. You can find time to enjoy time with your spouse!

Cook together! Shop together! Or, go food shopping early morning so you have your evening free.

Meal prep or use the crockpot to give you more time with your spouse.

If you and your hubby don't regularly have date nights or spend quality time with each other, why? What can you do to change that?

In this chapter's Resources, I have two lists for you. One for date night ideas out of the house. The other, date night ideas at home. Some cost money, some are free or cheap. Your homework this week is to schedule a date night for this week or next.

I strongly encourage you to have a date night every week or every other week. It will do wonders for your marriage.

ACTS OF SERVICE

Acts of service is simply doing something for your spouse that you know they would like for you to do. Cooking a meal, washing dishes, taking out the garbage, mowing the lawn, changing the baby's diaper, and painting the bedroom, etc.

If this is your spouse's primary love language, nothing speaks as loudly as these acts of service. You may give him or her words of affirmation, but they are thinking, "Cut the talk. If you loved me, you would do something around here." For them, actions truly speak louder than words.

Jesus gave a simple but profound illustration of expressing love by an act of service when He washed the feet of His disciples. In a culture where people wore sandals and walked on dirt streets, it was customary for the servant of the house to wash the feet of guests as they arrived. When we translate this into a marriage, it means that we will do acts of service to express love to our spouse. Why not choose one to express love to your spouse today?

It's funny, but one of my husband's favorite acts of service that I do for him seems so small to me, but he loves it. I make sure that I always have his favorite (homemade) sweet tea in the fridge and have a cold glass of it waiting on the counter for him when he comes home. So small, yet he appreciates it so much.

It's like the old hallmark commercial "little things mean a lot". What are the little things you do or can do to show your husband how much you love him?

WORDS OF AFFIRMATION

If you have taken the 5 love languages quiz and found that your love language (or one of them) or one of your husband's love languages is words of affirmation, this work book will help you to develop that love language.

Even if you have found that words of affirmation were not one of your or your husband's primary love languages, I encourage you to read and complete this section of chapter 2, anyway. Everyone can benefit from being spoken kind words. The Bible says:

Proverbs 16:24 Pleasant words are a honeycomb, Sweet to the soul and healing to the bones.

Job 4:4 "Your words have helped the tottering to stand, And you have strengthened feeble knees.

Proverbs 15:1 A gentle answer turns away wrath, But a harsh word stirs up anger.

There are dozens and dozens of references to kind words in scripture. Clearly, God wants us to speak kindly to everyone, but especially our spouses.

Kind words can be expressed about many things and for many reasons. I've outlined the main 5 for you below with some examples:

1) Humility

2) Gratitude and Appreciation

3) Encouragement

4) Empathy

5) Respect and admiration

Humility

We don't do this as often as we should, but when we remember, my husband and I tell each other three Things. First, we tell each other (1) what we regret doing (or not doing) that day (2) what we're thankful for and (3) how we know the other person is "the one." These three things are a great way to end our day. We give thanks, we apologize for any wrongs and we reaffirm why we love each other.

Sometimes, in the heat of a moment, it is tough to admit you were wrong. These three things give us that opportunity. If you're having a hard time saying sorry, a note is a great way to do so. And there's nothing like a humble heart to break down a wall between two people.

EXAMPLES OF WORDS OF HUMILITY:

I regret/I'm sorry for . . .

Next time, I'll try to . . .

I could've done ___ better today . . .

You must have been (upset, confused, etc.) when I . . .

Gratitude and Appreciation

Nothing fills me up more than hearing my husband notice all the little things I do for him. Whether he sends me a quick thank you text for the delicious lunch I made, or he lists all the actions he appreciates during "Three Things," his thankfulness shows me that he doesn't take me for granted. Simple heartfelt gratitude gives extra meaning and purpose to our daily actions.

Be specific. It's a wonderful gift to show the other person how much you care about his or her unique role in your life.

EXAMPLES OF WORDS OF APPRECIATION:

I appreciate that you . . .

I couldn't ___ today if it weren't for you . . .

I am thankful that you . . .

I'm glad to have you as my (mom, sister, friend, etc.) because . . .

Encouragement

Apart from being a small business owner, ministry leader, and consultant, I'm also a wife and mother. Needless to say, there are a lot of areas in my life where I have opportunities to fall short. Even on days when I feel most successful, I question whether I could have done this or that better. My husband puts my self-doubts at ease when he tells me how much he believes in me and my abilities.

He knows when I am struggling or stressed and will often send me a quick text or call to check in on me and let me know he's thinking of me. He is also my biggest cheerleader with my growing business and ministry. He tells me often how much he believes in me and knows that I am on the path God has ordained me to be on.

I often encourage him, too. He is also a business owner and sometimes, things get rough or our adult children make what we feel are incredibly stupid choices I'll let him know that I am proud of him or that I think he is a great dad. Who knew that taking a minute to give someone a little encouragement could change a person's entire attitude for the rest of the day?

EXAMPLES OF WORDS OF ENCOURAGEMENT:

I believe in you because . . .

It impressed me when you . . .

The good news is . . .

When you need something to lift your spirits, just remember that . . .

Empathy

I think a lot of people struggle with empathy. It's hard if we haven't been in someone else's "shoes". Words of affirmation are a way to show someone that you understand or at least are trying to understand. It's comforting for me to have someone to experience your struggles with. When my husband tells me that he recognizes my sacrifices and sufferings, I feel closer to him. I feel like someone is helping me carry the weight on my shoulders.

A great way to empathize with someone's emotions, even if you don't quite understand them, is to reflect on what they may be feeling or thinking. Paraphrase what you can tell they might be going through.

EXAMPLES OF WORDS OF EMPATHY:

It must be really tough that you . . .

I can't imagine how hard it must be for you to . . .

That sounds . . . Is that right?

I could see how you would feel that way because . . .

Respect and Admiration

Whenever my husband and I ask couples for their secrets to a long and happy marriage, respect is among the top three answers. We may respect and admire the people we love, but how often do we express it with words? When my husband builds me up with concrete reasons of why he respects me, I can't help but feel loved. In this way, it encourages me to stay true to myself, to grow, and to continue to follow my dreams and goals as an individual. It moves me to recognize the strengths I have that I may take for granted, especially in the throes of daily life. It also reminds me of the complementary aspects of our personalities, as we often admire most in others what we tend to lack in ourselves.

Show your loved one that you respect him or her by speaking politely and giving compliments. Be specific and sincere. When you do disagree on something, refrain from making judgmental statements. Reach out by asking questions or offering to talk about it more instead. In the end, it's OK to have differences. As an act of love, words of affirmation should be focused on the other person, not on yourself.

EXAMPLES OF WORDS OF RESPECT:

Great job . . .

I'm so thankful to have you in my life because . . .

I wish I could ___ the way you do.

It makes me happy when you . . .

I'm proud of you for . . .

PHYSICAL TOUCH

Intimacy is defined as: the state of being intimate, familiarity

Whereas sex is defined as: sexual activity, including specifically sexual intercourse.

Unfortunately, many people confuse the two. They are related, but certainly not the same.

We can be intimate, without having sexual intercourse. We can have sex without being intimate.

Intimacy, as defined above, is about familiarity. How well we know our spouse. How comfortable we are around them. It can be physical touch, but it is so much more.

For some, physical touch is a love language, for others, it's not as important.

For me, physical touch is huge, but not necessarily sex. It's the holding hands, the kiss when my husband arrives home from work. It's the arm around me while we watch a movie. The stroke of my cheek when he tells me goodnight.

Sex. Well, that's a whole different story. The word can conjure up so many different emotions from fear, dread, joy, pleasure depending on many factors.

As Christians, we know that sex was designed by God for married couples to enjoy (and to procreate, but that's another story), but it's never just that easy.

Whether you have an active sex life with your spouse or there are months in between "activity", there are a few things that should come before the physical act of sex. Chiefly, intimacy should come before sex. We will dive deeper into intimacy and sex in chapter 7.

Prayer:

Our Father, today, we praise You with our whole heart. We praise Your marvelous works. We will be glad and rejoice in You; we will sing praises to Your Name.

Father, You command us to love one another, for love comes from You. Anyone who loves is Your child and knows You. Those who do not love do not know You, for You are love. You have shown how much You loved us by sending Your one and only Son, Jesus, into the world so that we might have eternal life through Him. This is real love – not that we loved You, but You loved us and sent Your Son as a sacrifice to take away our sins. Thank You, Jesus, for giving Your life for ours. We were not worthy, yet, You made us worthy to love and know You. Thank You! Today, we confess that we will love You with all of our hearts, souls, strength and minds, and we will love our neighbor as we love ourselves.

Father, show me how to strengthen my relationship with You and my husband _____.

Lord, give me an open heart as I go through this study. Help me to put you at the center of my marriage. God, give me eyes to see where I can show my husband love. True love, Agape love. In Your precious Holy name. Amen.

Action Plan:

- List three ways that you can show agape love to your husband and choose at least one to do this week
- Take the Love Languages quiz online at: http://www.5lovelanguages.com/profile/ (Ask your husband to take the quiz, as well)
- Pray over your findings and choose at least one act from each of your husband's love languages to perform this week.
- When you notice your husband loving you with a sacrificial and unconditional love. Thank him and journal about it. Praise God for your husband and his love for you. (This is important. We get so tied up in the minutia and stress of everyday living that we can fail to notice or appreciate our husband's love through words or action. By journaling about it and thanking God, you are developing a grateful heart which goes a long way in cultivating a God centered marriage)

Study Guide:

Describe a time when you witnessed the unconditional love of agape.

Describe a time when you experienced the unconditional love of agape.

Describe a time when your spouse showed you the unconditional love of agape.

How would you describe the difference between agape and phileo (or philia)?

How is God's love for us both sacrificial and unconditional?

How does that knowledge make you feel?

How can you show agape to your husband?

What does agape look like for a husband to show to his wife?

What about a wife to her husband?

How will you, as a couple, make God's Word a priority in your life and in your marriage?

When you have completed your quiz, list your and your husband's top 3 love languages here:

My love languages:

My husband's love languages:

Did any of the answers surprise you? Why or why not?

Does knowing your husband's love languages motivate you to change how you show him love?

What action steps are you going to take to use your husband's love languages to better show him love?

If you have a love language of gifts, what are some gifts that you would love to receive from your spouse?

If your spouse has a love language of gifts, ask him what he would like to receive.

What are some of the best gifts that you have received from your husband? Why were they so special to you?

Ask your husband the same question.

Is acts of service one of your or your spouse's primary love languages?

What are some acts of service that your spouse does for you that you truly appreciate?

Ask your husband what are some of his favorite acts of service that you do for him?

Brainstorm what acts of service you can do for your spouse this week.

Were words of affirmation one of your or your husband's primary love languages?

Do you regularly use words of affirmation to your husband?

If so, what impact do you think it has on your marriage?

If not, why don't you?

What impact do you think adding more words of affirmation will make on your marriage?

Does your husband speak words of affirmation to you?

If he did or does, how does it make you feel?

If he doesn't, I encourage you to talk to him about it.

Which of the 5 main areas of words of affirmation do you struggle with the most?

Which come easiest to you?

Why do you think that is?

What steps are you going to take to add words of affirmation to your marriage?

Chapter 3

What it Means to Be a Submissive Wife & Your Husband as Your First Ministry

A submissive wife. Are you kidding me? You want me to be my husband's slave? You want me to do everything he tells me to do and bow to him? I hear it all the time from women in online groups and forums. Whether it is assumed that the wife is to be a passive participant while her husband bosses her around or that she is to wait on him hand and foot while he does nothing and barks orders at her, it's a common misconception. Being a submissive wife does NOT mean that you are your husband's slave. To better understand what it means to be a submissive wife, let's take a closer look at the definition of the word. The word submissive is defined as: inclined or ready to submit or to put oneself under authority of another.

Bible.org says The Greek word Paul uses here is a military term meaning to put oneself in rank under another. God has ordained the principle of authority and submission in a number of different spheres: Citizens are to be subject to civil authorities (Rom. 13:1; Titus 3:1); slaves to their masters (Col. 3:22; Titus 2:9); church members to their leaders (1 Cor. 16:16; Titus 2:15; Heb. 13:17); children to their parents (Col. 3:20); and wives to their husbands (Eph. 5:22, 24; Col. 3:18; Titus 2:5; 1 Pet. 3:1). Every time the New Testament speaks to the role of wives, the command is the same: "Be subject to your husband."

Notice that describes submit as to be subject to. It does not say to be a slave to. To be submissive means to put yourself under the authority of your husband. In Ephesians 5:25, husbands are instructed to, "Love your wives, just as Christ also loved the church and gave Himself up for her." and in Ephesians 5:22, wife are told to, "Be subject to your own husbands as to the Lord." When a husband loves his wife as he loves the church and when women focus on their role to love and be subject to their husbands, according to scripture, marriage is loving, kind and harmonious, not abusive or a slave to master relationship.

Submission is a voluntary action by the wife. It is a God-driven desire to please your husband and act under his authority just as Christians are to act under the authority of the church.

While the husbands are to be the head of the household, the wife is not commanded to keep her mouth shut and never give her opinion on matters. She "speaks with wisdom and faithful instruction is on her tongue" (Proverbs 31:26) The wife can and should share her thoughts on important family and household topics with her husband but she should do so in a way that is pleasing to God. How? Choose your words carefully. Don't argue or try to prove your point just to be right. In a biblical marriage, the wife is the helpmeet of her husband. She should support him and give counsel. Ultimately, he is to make decisions based on sound biblical knowledge AND his wife's wisdom and faithful instruction. The wife is to support her husband and back his decisions even when she doesn't agree.

While the Bible instructs women to confront their husbands regarding their sin :

1 Peter 3:1 NIV

3 Wives, in the same way submit yourselves to your own husbands so that, if any of them do not believe the word, they may be won overwithout words by the behavior of their wives,

it does not say that women should be quiet and use only their actions. The key is HOW women use their words. True submission is demonstrated in both words and actions. Wives are to submit to their husbands as husbands are to submit to God.

Often, I hear women lamenting that being submissive doesn't work in today's world or that the Bible was written thousands of years ago and that those same principles don't make sense today. I say "nonsense"! While division of labor in the home has changed drastically throughout history and varies from home to home and marriage to marriage, the Bible, and God, are unchanging. Husbands are still to be the authority in the home and act as the spiritual leader.

Submissiveness is not timidity, it is not servility, it is not subservience, it is not docility, it is not degrading, it is not a sign of weakness.

Submission is a sign of strength, not of weakness and a greater degree of submission requires a greater degree of strength of personal character.

Submitting to your husband means:

- Supporting his decisions even when you don't agree
- Following his spiritual lead

- Having a heart toward satisfying your husband

Being a submissive wife does not mean:

- Being physically or emotionally abused
- Being forced to do things that are illegal or immoral just because your husband told you to
- Going against God's wishes over that of your husband (For example, if a non-believing husband tells his wife that she cannot attend church)

Are you submissive to your husband? I pray that this chapter's resources will give you a better understanding of what it means to submit to your husband. I am praying for you, sister!

30 Ways to Submit to Your Husband Each Day of Your Marriage

1. Before you submit to your husband, submit yourself to the Lord. Submission to God is your northern star. He will give you the motivation, your guidance, and a right heart for submitting to your husband. God is the head of your marriage.

   (Matthew 22:37-38; 1 Chronicles 16:25-27; Exodus 20:1-3.)

2. Remember that your husband is your beloved and you are commanded to love him and care for him as you desire for him to love and care for you.

   (Song of Songs 2:3; Matthew 7:12)

3. Pray for a God to give you a greater understanding of what He wants you to do in your marriage and both your role and your husband's role in your union.

    (Jeremiah 33:3; James 1:5)

4. Acknowledge that God should always be in control of your marriage and that marriage should not be a power struggle.

    (2 Chronicles 20:6)

5. Remember that God has placed your husband in this position of leadership in your marriage and over you as his wife.

    (Ephesians 5:22-24)

6. Acknowledge the Holy Spirit's role in your faith, in your marriage and in your life. He has the power to change hearts and direct both of you. Always trust and rely on Him to lead you. Remember, your submission to your husband is "as to the Lord"

    (Ephesians 5:22).

7. Trust the Lord and that He has a plan for you. Take each step in faith in Him.

    (Proverbs 3:5-6)

8. When sharing your opinions with your husband, do so respectfully and using words that build up rather than tear down.

    (Ephesians 5:33)

9. When decisions are to be made and you don't agree with your husband, remember that it is his job to make the final decision. Trust that God's will be done.

    (Titus 2:4-5)

10. No matter how strong the urge to take control, remember that God is in control and you are to follow your husband's lead.

    (Luke 9:23; Romans 8:9)

11. Pray for your husband.

    (Ephesians 1:16-19)

12. Pray with your husband.

    (Matthew 18:20)

13. Recognize that your husband is also the spiritual head of household. Allow him to lead in family or couple's devotions. If he does not currently do this or he is resistant to it, pray that God will give him the desire to lead in this way.

    (Ephesians 5:22-30)

14. Never undermine your husband's authority by going behind his back to do something you know he would not like.

    (Ephesians 5:22, 33)

15. Put him above all others (except God)...with your time, your service, your choices, your decisions and your love.

    (Ephesians 5:31)

16. Consider your husband's perspective in all of your small daily personal decisions. For bigger decisions, talk with your husband, ask his opinion and ask him to pray with and for you to make the best possible decision.

    (Matthew 19:4-6; Matthew 18:20)

17. Give yourself freely to your husband physically and intimately.

    (1 Corinthians 7:2-4; Song of Songs 4:16)

18. When he wants to talk, listen. When he doesn't, accept it. Men are not as verbal as women. That is how God designed us.

    (James 1:19-20; Ephesians 4:2-3)

19. Give him grace. The role of husband is not an easy one.

    (Proverbs 22:11; Romans 16:20; Ephesians 5:25-27)

20. Humble yourself.

    (1 Peter 3:8; Psalm 25:9)

21. Deny your own wants and desires when it is conflicting with his.

    (Philippians 2:3-4)

22. Respect your husband. Respect is an inseparable part of submission. Respect the fact that he is a sinner too and needs the Lord just like you do. Respect his opinion as valid and valuable. Respect his feelings. (He has them even if he doesn't express them). Respect his role as head over you and your family.

    (Proverbs 31:23; Ephesians 5:33)

23. Take care of the things he asks you to take care of. This is working together in oneness.

   (Proverbs 31:27)

24. Respect his desires and wishes even when he isn't able to be a part of something. Such instances might include an illness, being at work, travel away from home, or being unable to contact him. Knowing your husband's ways of doing things, his preferences, his wishes and what he has led both of you to do in the past will help in making those daily decisions to submit to his authority. And when unsure, pray for the wisdom and strength to make the right choice.

   (Proverbs 31:11-12; Colossians 3:23-24)

25. Be careful not to use these situations as a way to take advantage to get your own way. This only separates you and destroys oneness.

   (Leviticus 25:17)

26. Don't be resentful, get angry, pout or sulk when you don't get your own way. In addition, do not badmouth your husband to others.
   (Titus 3:1-2)

27. Give your insecurity and fears over to the Lord.

   (Isaiah 41:10; Psalm 118:6)

28. Pray continually God to give wisdom and direction to your husband so he will lead you and your family in God's ways and always make the right decisions for you.

   (Colossians 4:2; Ephesians 1:17)

29. We are to cleave from our mother and father when we marry. God has given authority over you to your husband in place of your parents.given that place to your husband. You should still love and care for your parents, but you are no longer in submission to them.

    (Genesis 2:24; Ephesians 5:23)

30. If there is something your husband wants you to do that you believe goes against the Lord and His ways, respectfully and lovingly go to him and show him in God's Word why you believe this. And pray for God to change his mind. But if he refuses to change, you must respectfully refuse to submit to his sinful desire and choose instead to submit to the Lord. A biblical wife always submits first to the Lord.

    (Acts 4:19-20; Proverbs 31:30; Ephesians 4:14-15)

31. Obviously, submission to an unbelieving husband is a little more difficult. He does not rely on God to lead him. He will make choices that do not follow God's ways. And he will have difficulty choosing to do right over choosing to follow his feelings. But even believing husbands do this at times. And so the answer is always the same—the bottom line is submitting to the Lord, and inasmuch as your husband submits to God's ways, you are able to submit to him.

    (1 Peter 3:1-4; Colossians 3:18)

Of course, this isn't an exhaustive list. What other ways can you think of to demonstrate submission to your husband?

Prayer

Dear Lord,

Please help me to understand what it means to submit, to You, Lord and to my husband. The world tells us that submission is a negative thing In a day where Your ways are not accepted, please help me to remain strong and live how You want me to. Show me what it means to submit in marriage. Help me remain humble and willing to submit to my husband daily. Please help us to submit our hearts to You. Lord, thank You for Your grace that operates in and through me so I can live as You've called me to live. Your Word says I am to submit to my husband as to You (Ephesians 5:22). I need Your help to walk that out. Shield me from outside influences that say I'm weak for walking in submission. It takes strength to yield. Grace to stand strong in adversity. Help me to be influenced by You alone. To be a voice of godly influence to my husband but to always submit to his lead. Give me eyes to see the blessing and protection of submission. Help us to walk in marriage unity as we align our hearts to Your purpose. In Your Son's Holy Name. Amen.

Action Plan

- Choose three of the 30 ways to submit to your husband. Pray that God works in you to submit to your husband in this way. Make a true effort to improve in these areas.
- Recommit to being a biblical, submissive wife.
- Complete the 10 Way I commit to being a submissive wife to my husband. Stick this in your Bible or War Room and pray over them, including the accompanying scripture.

Study Guide

Do you agree or disagree with the above about being a submissive wife?

Do you consider yourself a submissive wife?

What does being a submissive wife mean to you in the context of biblical instruction.

Is there an area of your marriage that you struggle with in being submissive to your husband?

What can you do to change that?

What is God telling you about submission?

Chapter 4

The Art of Communication

It's time to address an area that can be a minefield for many couples, even Christian couples. Communication.

Recently, a lifestyle website polled 100 mental health professionals and found that communication problems were cited as the most common factor that leads to divorce (65 percent), followed by couples' inability to resolve conflict (43 percent).

They survey also found that men and women have different communication complaints. Seventy percent of the experts surveyed said that men cite nagging and complaining as the top communication problem in their marriage. Women's top complaint was that their spouse doesn't validate their opinions or feelings enough, according to 83 percent of experts.

This week, we are going to discuss communication marriage. How the Bible commands that we communicate and tips for positive communication.

In the next chapter, we will explore conflict and fighting fairly.

Are you ready to dive in?

"We just don't communicate like we used to. My husband never talks to me." "My wife is always trying to get me to talk. " Sound familiar? Probably so. Most marriages seem to have some level of communication issues and when communication breaks down, barriers build up, and marriages can break down.

God created humans for communication, particularly in marriage. Marital communication is to reflect the intimate communication of God Himself. And, as we were created in God's image, we were created for communication.

So why is communication so difficult? There are dozens of reasons that communication in marriage is difficult to navigate. Sometimes it is due to how we were raised. We may have had parents who didn't communicate with each other or with us. A generation before us, there was an adage that children are to be seen and not heard.

In addition, we live in a culture where people are continually isolated. We see kids spending hours playing video games or couples watching televisions in separate rooms, but I think one of the worst culprits is our telephones. How many times have you seen couples in a restaurant with their faces down on their phones and not communicating with the person across the table from them?

Life gets messy. We have pressures from jobs, ministries and errands. Schedules, themselves can serve to isolate couples when they simply lack quality time together. When they finally do end up in the same room, they are tired and, in many cases, still thinking about the outside pressures that life brings.

Finally, some spouses experience the fear of rejection or of showing their emotions if they communicate openly and honestly.

Good grief! That's a lot of barriers to effective communication in a marriage, isn't it? No wonder communication is the highest cited reason for divorce in our society.

So what do we do about it?

The easy answer is to talk to each other. I know, I know, that sounds simplistic and it is, but, yet, it isn't. In our reading material for this lesson, we'll dive into some strategies that you can use to help foster positive communication with your spouse.

So, now we recognize (if we haven't already) that communication issues are the number one reason for divorce in today's culture. You, yourself, may be experiencing a breakdown of communication with your husband. Perhaps you have been praying that God would allow him to open up to you or that the fighting would stop.

I'm going to share with you some strategies for improved communication with your husband as well as the biblical truths that surround these strategies.

First, let's look at four ways to immediately improve communication in a marriage:

1. Know your spouse
2. Recognize the differences between men and women
3. Learn to listen
4. Use Words that Build Up

Know your Spouse

1 Peter 3:7

Husbands, in the same way be considerate as you live with your wives, and treat them with respect as the weaker partner and as heirs with you of the gracious gift of life, so that nothing will hinder your prayers.

When we are familiar with someone, their likes and dislikes, their "pet peeves" and their communication styles, communication becomes less like a battlefield and more like a meeting of the minds.

Do you notice that your husband is tense when he gets home from work? That might not be the best time to discuss how he doesn't help around the house.

Has he complained that you nag him? You may not feel that you are nagging, but something in your words or his hearing of them is bringing that feeling up for him. Consider how you share your thoughts and emotions (more on that below).

How do you get to know your spouse? By observing them and by talking to them. Ask your husband if there is a time of day or day of the week that he would be open to talking. Ask him how he prefers that you ask him to get something done around the house.

As a mom, I've always "run a tight ship". Daily, my children received a list of the chores they were to do. They knew they had to complete them before any social activities.

When I married my husband, I started to give him daily chore lists and guess what? He never did them. When I finally inquired as to why (but not before getting irritated and annoyed with him), he told me that he felt like I was treating him as a child when I did this. Well, I guess I was.

How did he want to know what I needed him to do? He said to just ask him nicely. (One of my husband's love languages is words of affirmation). I started to ask him to get household chores done in this way "Hey honey, thank you for taking out the garbage last night. I really appreciate it. Do you think you could shampoo the living room carpet when you get a chance? It's getting pretty crummy and you always do such a great job with it"

See the difference? I was building him up (words of affirmation) and asking him nicely. I wasn't dictating to him what he NEEDED to do like I did the kids.

Recognize the Difference Between Men and Women

Colossians 3:19

Husbands, love your wives and do not be harsh with them.

God created men and women differently as we have discussed in the Introduction lesson of this course.

Men and women were created with not just physical and emotional differences, but communication differences, as well. These differences, when not recognized, can cause great sources of communication breakdowns.

Women tend to share their feelings and thoughts more easily, often with a close friend. Men are more goal or outcome oriented. They tend not to talk about feelings with their friends, but are more likely to talk about surface issues (sports, politics, weather, business, etc.) and do activities alongside their friends.

Both women and men have a tendency to ignore the gender differences and talk with our spouses in the way we would a friend. This can cause hurt feelings and resentment.

God created us differently and in ways that are to be honored. We were not created to try to change the other person to be more like us, be it in emotions, views or how we communicate.

Learn to Listen

James 1:19

My dear brothers and sisters, take note of this: Everyone should be quick to listen, slow to speak and slow to become angry,

In my first college course on communication, we learned how to employ "active listening". It may seem cliché, or something that a therapist would do, but it is truly effective, particularly in marital communication.

People have an innate desire to be heard and acknowledged. As they saying goes, God gave us one mouth and two ears for a reason.

To practice "active listening", let your spouse speak. Don't interrupt them, don't "but" them, and don't wander off thinking of your reply before they get their words out.

When your husband shares something with you or you are having a disagreement, repeat back what he said to ensure that you fully understand.

"I heard you say that you are frustrated when I don't get the laundry done and let it pile up." Or "It sounds like you are upset with me for forgetting to mail the car payment" Then ask how they believe you can fix it. It may be obvious but allowing your husband to be heard and acknowledged will edify him and improve both your communication and your marriage.

Use Word That Build Up

Ephesians 4:29

Do not let any unwholesome talk come out of your mouths, but only what is helpful for building others up according to their needs, that it may benefit those who listen.

Whether your spouse has a love language of words of affirmation or not, no one likes to be cut down by words. We've all heard, as youngsters, the chant "Sticks and stones can break my bones, but words can never hurt me". Friends, it is just not true. Words can hurt deeply. Even words that don't have the intention of hurting can leave wounds.

One way to improve this is to use another effective communication tool called "I statements". Instead of saying "You never spend time with me" or "You never listen to me!", reframe the statements to "I statements" and include how the "offense" make you feel. Own the statement, don't project it on your spouse.

For example, instead of "You never spend time with me" can be rephrased "I feel lonely when we don't spend time together" Or "It hurts me when I try to discuss something with you and I feel as though you aren't listening to me".

In these examples, you are sharing how you feel, owning the statement, but not accusing your spouse. This type of communication allows for open discussion of feelings and resolutions.

Another way to do this is to use an effective technique often used in performance reviews at companies. It is called the "sandwich method". In this method, you "sandwich" a negative message with two positive ones. For example, "Honey, I love that you have hobbies that you enjoy and I think that spending time with friends is important, but I would love if you could let me know in advance of your golf outings so we don't have any conflicts with the kids schedules. You are such a great dad I know you don't want to miss Billy's games".

How could you use the sandwich method to build up instead of tear down with your husband?

Prayer

Dear God,

Thank You for my husband. Thank You for the relationship that we have, although I always pray that it continues to grow! Thank You for working in our lives and leading us through transformation! I lift up my marriage to You and ask that You help my husband and I grow in the area of communication. I pray that we can talk to each other kindly and respond in love to each other. Help us not to be selfish or pursue things that will only benefit us, but rather help us to keep each other in mind. I pray that our marriage and other marriages would be blessed by having an awesome communication line! May Your words be on our lips daily. May Your wisdom and your encouragement flow through us affirming our spouses in Jesus' name AMEN!

Action Plan

At the end of each day or week (discuss what works best with your husband), ask each other the following questions:

Is there anything that I need to apologize for? (or: Did I do anything that hurt you?)

Is there anything you need from me that you're not getting?

How can I be a better spouse?

What are you looking most forward to tomorrow (or this week)?

What are you dreading or not looking forward to tomorrow (or this week)?

LISTEN to each other and use what you have learned to be a better spouse in the coming days and weeks.

Study Guide

What was new a new concept or stood out to you in this chapter?

In what ways were you challenged or encouraged? Were there any parts that you did not agree with?

Peter said to dwell with your spouse according to knowledge (1 Peter 3:7). What intimate knowledge about your mate have you discovered that is especially helpful when communicating?

What intimate knowledge about yourself would help your mate better communicate with you?

How will you continue to cultivate this intimate knowledge in the marriage relationship, especially when life becomes busy with work, kids, ministry, etc.?

It is very common for couples to have communication problems due to the difference in how God created male and female. Are there any communication issues in your marriage that you believe are due to gender differences?

How does a miscommunication often begin and what triggers it?

What ways have you experienced the importance of abiding in Christ for communication?

After completing this chapter, how do you feel God is calling you to pray for your marriage?

Chapter 5

Resolving Conflict and Forgiveness

In the previous chapter, we discussed communication in a marriage and ways to improve communication for a happier home. In this chapter, we will expand upon that by discussing how to reduce and resolve conflict. We'll also discuss forgiveness and what it means to a marriage.

When humans received a nature of sin during the fall, we became prone to conflict. The sin of pride is often the culprit. Conflict is inevitable, but how we handle it is the difference between a successful, God-honoring marriage and a broken marriage.

There are many ways to avoid and handle conflict, but these three are the key and, I think the foundation for the remaining seven:

1. Remembering the God is the head of our marriage
2. Loving our spouses more than anything after God
3. Practicing forgiveness

We'll talk about the otherseven in our reading today. But, for now, let's take a look at the three I mentioned.

1. Remembering that God is the head of our marriage. In Ephesians 5:25-27, we read "Husbands, love your wives, just as Christ loved the church and gave himself up for her 26 to make her holy, cleansing[a] her by the washing with water through the word, 27 and to present her to himself as a radiant church, without stain or wrinkle or any other blemish, but holy and blameless."

In several of the couple's devotions that my husband and I have completed, we've read that marriage is not about happiness; it is about holiness.

When we place God at the center of our marriages and learn more about the love of our Heavenly Father, we learn how to model this love with our husbands.

2. Loving our spouses more than anything after God. When we love someone, we don't like to see them hurt. Conflict causes hurt. By avoiding conflict and properly resolving it, according to biblical principles, we are protecting our spouses from the hurt that conflict brings. Love is more than a feeling or emotion. It is an action. Loving our spouses means loving them enough to avoid conflict, avoid hurting them and putting their needs and wants above ours.

Remember that loves covers a multitude of sins.

3. Practicing forgiveness. Forgiveness is the choice to give up the right for revenge, resentment and the need to be right. Forgiveness allows for healing and resolution. It promotes reconciliation. Forgiveness doesn't mean that you forget about the "offense". It doesn't mean that you condone the behavior. It means that that your spouse is more important to you than the mistakes he made.

When God comes first in your marriage, you are better equipped to resolve any issues that inevitably arise in a marriage.

Let's head over to this week's reading material to learn more about handling conflict in a Christian marriage.

Now that we've looked at conflict in marriage and three of the keys to avoiding it and handling it. Let's take a look at the other seven:

Having a Joyful Attitude

Some people are born with their "dukes" up ready for a right. Maybe you are this way. Perhaps, you spent your childhood years always defending yourself and this posture comes naturally. Or maybe, your fear of rejection prompts this readiness for conflict.

Whatever the reason, developing a joyful attitude is required to avoid potential conflict with your husband. If conflict is your natural response, this may be a bit difficult for you to change, but God is your stronghold and He will help you.

God often uses conflict to point out areas of sin. Instead of getting frustrated about conflict in your marriage, thank God for the conflict and ask Him to reveal your sin in it. Conflict is an opportunity to grow as a person, as a wife and as a daughter of The One True King.

Remembering That Marriage Isn't Disposable

We live in a disposable society. Disposable diapers, paper plates, heck even microwaves are only built to last a few years now. Sadly, many people view marriage as disposable, as well. When issues arise and they feel the marriage is broken, it's time to throw it away.

Divorce grieves our Heavenly Father. We vowed to love in sickness and in health, for better or for worse. And, yes, my friends, we may feel that we have more than our fair share of "for worse" days, but God designed marriage to be for a lifetime.

We aren't to throw in the towel when things get tough.

As I mentioned above, conflict points out sin. It also refines character and faith. In James 1:3-4, we read:

3 because you know that the testing of your faith produces perseverance. 4 Let perseverance finish its work so that you may be mature and complete, not lacking anything.

We are to persevere through conflict as conflict teaches us to trust God more. The Lord helps us to develop peace, patience, and joy, regardless of our circumstances. He helps us to grow in character as we "let perseverance finish its work."

I'm not saying to persevere by "rolingl over" and taking it. I'm saying to put in the hard work to avoid and resolve conflict and give it to God to handle the rest. While we are on the subject, if your marriage involves physical or emotional abuse, go to a safe place and seek Christian counseling immediately. When I talk about "taking it", I'm talking about disagreements. Perseverance is not avoiding sharing your opinions or feelings or never expressing hurts. It's not giving up when times get tough.

Recognizing That Marriage is a Lot Like Farming

I'm not trying to make light of marriage or simplify it. Marriage can be tough, we all know that. What I am saying is that throughout Scripture, God uses farming or gardening to illustrate biblical truths. How we talk to and treat our spouses is a great example of that. Take a look at the following Bible verses:

Galatians 6:7

7 Do not be deceived: God cannot be mocked. A man reaps what he sows.

Luke 8:15

As for that in the good soil, they are those who, hearing the word, hold it fast in an honest and good heart, and bear fruit with patience.

What we sow, we reap. Are you expecting your husband to treat you with kindness and respect, but you treat him with avarice and disrespect?

Use words that build up, even in times of conflict and disagreement. These are seeds you are planting and the harvest will come.

If your husband is acting less than kind toward you, don't act spiteful. Instead love him even more.

I love this verse from Romans 12:19-21

19 Do not take revenge, my dear friends, but leave room for God's wrath, for it is written: "It is mine to avenge; I will repay,"[a] says the Lord. 20 On the contrary:

"If your enemy is hungry, feed him;

if he is thirsty, give him something to drink.

In doing this, you will heap burning coals on his head."[b]

21 Do not be overcome by evil, but overcome evil with good.

Pray that God will soften your husband's heart and that by seeing the love you demonstrate toward him, your husband will, in turn, treat you with the love and respect deserving of a godly wife.

If instead, you are nagging him, complaining that he doesn't spend time with you, etc, you will be pushing him away. (See the previous chapter on tips for rephrasing "complaints".

Sow what you wish to reap, dear sister!

What Happens in the Home Stays in the Home

It seems that nowadays people share every detail of their lives and their homes with everyone. We see selfies, photos of dinners and posts on Facebook with minutia of daily living.

When I was a child, my parents taught me that what happened in our home, stayed in the home. I wasn't to discuss family matters with anyone not in the family. In our culture, that is an old-fashioned, but incredibly important rule.

If you are having a disagreement with your husband, don't discuss it with your friend or neighbor. Talk to your husband about it.

While this verse in Matthew is directed toward dealing with conflict in the church, the lesson is applicable to marriage, as well:

Matthew 18:15

15 "If your brother or sister[a] sins,[b] go and point out their fault, just between the two of you. If they listen to you, you have won them over.

If the two of you are having an argument or he hurts your feelings, share it with him.

If you deem the offense unresolvable or your environment it is physically unsafe, seek a Christian counselor or your pastor to talk to.

When we are badmouthing our husband to others, not only is his reputation affected, but yours is, as well. It also pulls outsiders into private issues in your marriage.

Seeking Godly Counsel

I know that I just told you not to talk to others about the private affairs of your marriage and now I'm about to tell you to talk to others about it. A contradiction? No, not really.

There are times when resolving conflict with your husband is all you need to do. Good old fashioned discussion, prayer and hard work is all you need. Other times, however, it's not that easy.

When arguments are escalate and resolution seems unlikely, it's time to seek godly counsel.

In times of physical abuse or infidelity, you may need to seek godly counsel soon after the "offense" occurs as rarely do these types of problems resolve without deep work or counseling.

Who makes up your trusted cabinet of godly advisors? If you don't have one, discuss this with your husband before a need occurs. Perhaps it is an older couple from your church, either of your parents, a small group or Bible study leader, your pastor. Identify your "cabinet" before you need them.

Don't Sleep On It

Have you ever heard that bit of marital advice? Don't go to bed mad? It's actually from Scripture:

Ephesians 4:26-27

26 "In your anger do not sin"[a]: Do not let the sun go down while you are still angry, 27 and do not give the devil a foothold.

When we let an argument "stew" and go to sleep angry, we are giving the devil an opening in the door. If we don't talk through the issue with our husbands and instead, go to bed angry, we are holding resentment in our hearts and the evil one loves that!

While you may not be able to *resolve* a conflict before you go to bed, at least discuss it with your spouse and agree to disagree. Mostly importantly, PRAY about it together. It's hard to stay mad at someone when you pray with them. Praying together is a vulnerable act and sharing your heart to God with your spouse shows that you can't do it alone. You need God's help and are seeking it. It's tough to hold onto resentment when God is on the throne.

Sacrificing Our Needs For Our Husband's

Jesus paid the ultimate sacrifice for our sins. In fact, we, as Christians are to live a life of sacrifice modeled after Him. In Luke 9:23, we see 23 Then he said to them all: "Whoever wants to be my disciple must deny themselves and take up their cross daily and follow me.

What does taking up our cross daily mean in Christian marriage? This answer is also found in scripture:

Philippians 2:3-5

3 Do nothing out of selfish ambition or vain conceit. Rather, in humility value others above yourselves, 4 not looking to your own interests but each of you to the interests of the others.

5 In your relationships with one another, have the same mindset as Christ Jesus:

We are humans. We are selfish, but we are commanded to put the needs of others, especially those of our spouse before our own needs.

We need to worry more about the needs of our husband's than our own needs.

Let's say that your husband is offered a job 2000 miles away. Perhaps you don't want to leave your friends and family and the beautiful home that you spent the past five years decorating. Are your feelings selfish? Are you putting his needs before yours?

How can the two of you come to an agreement that honors God and His plan for marriage? Please don't mistake me here. I'm not saying that every situation (even the one illustrated above) is black and white. What I am saying is that often we need to step back and examine our own hearts? Are we being selfish? Are we putting our husband's needs first?

Love, marriage, involve sacrifices.

Of the ten areas described for avoiding and resolving conflict, which are the ones that God is shining a light on in your own heart and marriage?

Prayer

Dear Lord,

Thank You for the union of marriage and for my husband, specifically. We lift up to you the issue we are facing and ask for Your help in resolving it. Please put words in our mouths that will build up the other and not tear them down. Help us to listen to each other without judgement and remove any bitterness or resentment from our hearts. We know that you can heal anything, Father, including our marriage. Help us to see the other through Your eyes. We ask this in your Son's Holy Name. Amen.

Action Steps

If there are any unresolved issues in your marriage now, get on your knees and pray for God to help you and your husband resolve them.

Use this chapters printables to help you work through resolving conflict.

Study Guide

What was new or stood out to you in this chapter?

In what ways were you challenged or encouraged?

Most couples usually argue over similar topics. These are called "triggers". This might be when the woman shops, the man watches TV, somebody doesn't pick up after him or herself, etc.

Write down all the common triggers for arguments in your relationship.

Why do you think these triggers you or your husband to get angry?

Do you sow seeds of discord? Or are you speaking words that edify?

Who makes up your "cabinet" of godly advisors? If you don't have one, sit with your husband and agree on one. Be sure that both of you are in agreement on who should be a part of your cabinet.

Do you have a godly mentor? If not, prayerfully choose one. Someone who both you and your husband are comfortable with you sharing private marriage matters with.

After completing this chapter, how do you feel God is calling you to pray for your marriage?

Chapter 6

The Impact of Family on your Relationship

We have so much more to cover as we explore establishing God at the center of our marriages. In this chapter, we are going to talk about the effects of family on our marriages.

This may be a bit uncomfortable for some. You may recognize some of these pitfalls in your own relationship and God may convict you. Perhaps, you already know that one or more family members is holding a place they shouldn't have in your marriage.

I regularly hear from women about the effects that others have on their marriage. Sometimes it is a mother-in-law, sometimes their own mother or father. In other cases, it is their children. A marriage thrives when there are just three parties: God, Husband and Wife. No one else should enter the marriage union.

What often starts as advice giving, becomes bulldozing. Mothers place children as idols in their hearts. There are countless examples.

Genesis 2:24 states that "a man shall leave his father and his mother, and shall cleave to his wife,". In Hebrew the definition for leave is "to forsake dependence upon," "leave behind," "release," and "let go."

Cleave, is defined as to cling, cleave, keep close.

In Matthew, 19:6, Jesus reinforced this when he said:

6 So they are no longer two, but one flesh. Therefore what God has joined together, let no one separate.

In God's design for marriage, no one is to come between a husband and a wife. No one! Not in-laws, not mother, not father, not even the children you have made together, were meant to divide a couple who had vowed together in marriage. We are to leave, cleave and become one flesh.

I don't think that husbands or wives enter into a marriage with the expectation that others will have an active part in the marriage, but it happens all of the time. Wives regularly rely more and more on advice from someone else until that third party's opinion matters more than her husband's opinion. Husbands slowly allow their mothers to dictate to their wives until the wife is feeling less than an equal in her own marriage.

Children become the focal point and the husband's needs come last.

God has made it pretty clear that not only are we to leave our mothers and fathers when we marry and cleave or cling to our spouse, but He has also established our priorities:

- God

- Husband

- Everything else, even children and other family members.

In the rest of this chapter, we will look at each of these family relationships, the potential issues that may arise from each and how to address them to please God and increase marital joy.

Parents

We love our parents, I get it. I was Daddy's little girl and my husband might be described as a "Momma's Boy". Neither are bad things. In fact, good healthy relationships as children help us to form good healthy relationships as adults. The problem is that sometimes these relationships are not as healthy as they appear.

Throughout Scripture, we read that God intends for us to leave our parents and join with our husbands.

In fact, it is mentioned at least 8 times (that I am able to find).

Mark 10:7

'Therefore a man shall leave his father and mother and hold fast to his wife,

He also tell us that we are to:

Exodus 20:12

"Honor your father and your mother, that your days may be long in the land that the Lord your God is giving you.

So how do we achieve this balance?

God is not telling us not to have anything to do with our parents or in-laws. He is telling us that when we marry, our spouses come first (after Him, of course).

God knew, when He created humans, that our sinful nature would cause problems in our marriages. He knew that if we weren't careful, mothers and mothers in law and even children, could crack some marital foundations, intentional or not. I believe that is why He sprinkled this command liberally throughout His Word.

He wants us to be aware of the pitfalls and how we can avoid them. We are to honor our mothers and fathers but be submissive to our husbands and join with them.

Let's take a closer look at several relationships that can cause fractures in our covenant of marriage:

Mothers

Since most of participants in this course are women, I'm going to address the wives, first. We love our mothers. They are our first teachers and model how to be a wife and mothers.

Titus 2:4 says

4 Then they can urge the younger women to love their husbands and children,

God intended mothers to teach their daughters how to be good wives and mothers, themselves.

Unfortunately, some mothers do not relinquish their roles when their daughters marry. They continue to give advice (solicited or not) that may be in discordance with that of their son in law.

This becomes an issue when the daughter places her mother's advice over that of her husband.

Mothers are not bad guys. We just tend to have some difficulty letting our "babies" go. As a mother of grown children, myself, I regularly ask God to help me stay out of my children's business and marriages.

When asked, I will give advice, but always encourage them to discuss the issue with their spouse and come to an agreement together.

Later in this chapter, we will talk about setting healthy boundaries in all of our relationships that come in contact with our marriage.

Mothers in Law

Oooh boy. This is a touchy subject. Listen to any group of women talking and invariably you will hear quips about someone's mother-in-law. Mother's-in-law get a bad rap. Some deservedly so, others not so much. In a man's life, the two most important people are usually his wife and his mother. When a man marries, he is to leave his parents and become one with his wife.

For many mother's-in-law, this is tough. They birthed their son, they raised their son and now they are to willingly give their son to another woman. As a mother of two sons, I understand how hard this is. It can make many mother's-in-law jealous or feel that the woman is not good enough for her son. There are many reasons that mothers and daughters in law have contentious relationships. We won't get into that today, but I wanted to point out what a difficult relationship this can be.

You may have a mother in law that butts in to your marriage or tells you how to raise your kids. You may have a mother-in-law who is openly rude to you. Here's the thing: you can't change her. Only she can change herself. What you can do is to love her son and love her. God has commanded us to love others and this is a great example of ministering at home.

I have been blessed with an amazing mother-in-law. When describing her to others, I often say that if I wrote a job description for the perfect mother-in-law, she would far exceed it. She is kind, loving, compassionate. She may not always agree with me or the decisions that my husband and I make, but she never says so. She is thoughtful and has brought me gifts of plants and coffee mugs (two things I enjoy) and, during my recent cancer diagnosis and surgery, helped in numerous ways from preparing meals for us to letting the dogs out while I was in the hospital. I love spending time with her and learning from her. She is a strong Christian woman and one I admire as a Proverb 31 woman. She makes me want to be a better person, wife and daughter-in-law. Linda Lou is the perfect mother-in-law. I pray that our relationship honors Naomi and Ruth. (If you are not familiar with the story of Naomi and Ruth, you can read it in the Book of Ruth. It is a beautiful story of a mother in law and daughter in law, one that we can all learn from).

I know that I'm in the minority when it comes to amazing mother's-in-law, but perhaps you can impact your relationship with your mother-in-law a bit by taking some steps to love her a little more. When things get tough, think of Naomi and Ruth.

1 John 4:12

No one has ever seen God; if we love one another, God abides in us and his love is perfected in us.

Let your mother in law see Christ through your actions.

Soon, we'll look at establishing healthy boundaries and some tips for navigating family relationships within the context of your marriage. For now, since we can't change our mothers in law, only ourselves, here are ten tips for being a better daughter in law:

1. Speak only in kindness. Don't engage in arguments with your mother in law or complain about your husband to your mother in law.
2. Listen to her advice - even if you don't take it
3. Give her some leeway to spoil your kids (within reason)
4. Don't compare your in-laws to your parents
5. Go out of your way to help her (If she doesn't drive, offer to take her shopping.
6. Cultivate a relationship with her (Invite her for coffee or a movie, etc. Treat her as you would a girlfriend by calling just because or inviting her to do things with you)
7. Don't expect her to babysit all the time. Once in a while is fine and she may say that she doesn't mind, but don't take advantage of her.
8. Don't talk bad about your in-laws to your spouse
9. Talk to your husband and his family about holidays way in advance to avoid hurt feelings
10. Thank your in-laws for the way they raised your son.

Children

There is no love like that of a mother for her child. I adore my children as I'm sure you adore yours. That is a beautiful thing. Until that love becomes an idol or displaces the role of a husband to a wife.

I know. I know. This may seem harsh, but bear with me for a moment.

We are going to address two biblical realties here. First, God designed marriage to be a three cord strand, not a four, five or six or more cord strand. In biblical marriage, God comes first then our husbands and ourselves.

While we are to love and care for and nurture our children, we are not to place them before our husbands.

In 1 Peter 3 (CEV), we read:

3 If you are a wife, you must put your husband first.

This means serving your husband his dinner first. It means buying his favorite snacks at the grocery store. It means respecting his needs and his wishes. It means choosing his wants over your children's wants.

This practice not only pleases God as it is how He designed marriage, but it is modeling a good, God-honoring marriage for your children to see.

When we put our children first, they learn to be self-centered. The learn that, even though the Bible says that the husband should be the wife's first priority, mom doesn't put much stock in that.

The second biblical truth here is that mothers often make idols of their children. When nothing, not God, not their husband, comes before a child or children, those children become idols.

God blesses us with children and commands us to raise disciples.

If your mothering responsibilities are keeping you from your marital responsibilities, you may have made your children idols.

Other ways you may be making your children idols:

- Your mothering responsibilities prevent you from spending time in the Word and prayer
- You aren't disciplining your children for fear of getting them upset
- Your identity is solely in being so and so's mother, not so and so's wife or daughter of the King
- You are so busy and tired meeting your children's needs that you neglect your husband's needs

This is not an exhaustive list. I encourage you to pray and ask God to shine a light on any area of your marriage and motherhood that is not pleasing to Him. It may be uncomfortable but it is only through discomfort that we can grow and live a life that honors God.

While mothers, mother's in law and children are the most common relationships that interfere with a marriage, they are not the only ones. Prayerfully consider any relationship that you may be prioritizing or giving space to in your marriage. It could be a friendship, a relationship with a grandparent or other family member or even a boss or co-worker. Are you placing this person or relationship over your husband in word or deed? Ask God to identify any relationship that does not honor Him in your marriage.

5 Ways to Establish Healthy Family Boundaries to Protect Your Marriage

1. Establish your own home and your own family.

When you marry, you will have your own home and routines. For most of us, this means living in a place other than with your family. Of course, circumstances in life may require you to stay with your parents (or others) for a season, but, if at all possible, set up your own home, even if it is a one room apartment over a garage. We cannot leave and cleave if we are under the roof and authority of others.

In the same way, create new routines, new traditions and agree with your husband on the values and priorities that are important to the two of you.

2. Learn to depend on each other, not on your parents (or others)

As youngsters, we become dependent on our parents. We go to them for advice, for basic needs and for financial help. When we enter into marriage, this dependence needs to change from our parents to our spouses.

If we continue to depend on our parents (or in laws) for help, it undermines the convenant that we made in marriage. Them giving and you taking can cause expectations. For example, if your parents are continuing to give you money, they may expect a "say" in how you steward your finances or, by extension how you manage your own home.

In addition, the husband loses his foothold as head of household and he may lose respect from you or your family.

I'm not saying that you should never accept help, but only do so in the direst of circumstances as dependence on others can become a habit that is difficult to break and damaging to a marriage.

3.   Honor your mother and father

When we are commanded to leave our parents and cleave to our spouses, we are not commanded to break all ties with them. One of the ten commandments is to Honor thy father and mother. We can continue to honor them as married adults.

Seek to spend time with them both individually and as a couple. Thank them for their love, sacrifice and provision for you. When appropriate, ask for their wisdom and advice (careful not to place it over your husband's in importance).

4.   Stand Your Ground

Of the five ways to establish healthy family boundaries, this one is the most difficult for some. In some family relationships, manipulation becomes currency. Parents know, as before your husband, they raised you and know you best, what your triggers are and which buttons to push to get you to do what they want. Some parents take advantage of this. Guilt becomes the mechanism that they use to force you bend to their will.

You and your husband will need to be a united front. If the both of you agreed to have Thanksgiving dinner at your own house, but one of your parents is using guilt to convince you too attend the family dinner, instead, you will need to draw a line in the sand. Don't let guilt or manipulation rob your marriage of its foundation.

Husbands may need to shield their wives from manipulation by his family and wives may need to protect their husbands from the guilt by hers.

One way to ensure this foundation is not broken is by discussing and agreeing upon your own values, traditions and priorities as a couple then holding firm to your decisions.

5.   Protect and defend your spouse

Don't criticize your husband to your parents, or anyone, for that matter. Defend them when something negative is said about them.

Sadly, I hear this way too often. "My husband doesn't defend me or take my side when his mother is rude to me or criticizes me". Or "My father in law constantly puts me down and my wife never says a thing".

When you allow a family member to talk ill of your husband, you are damaging your vow of marriage. Even, my friend, if you happen to agree with the criticism, do not allow it. Do not condone gossip, slander or criticism of your spouse by anyone.

As a married couple, we are to protect our spouses from any threat, real or perceived. Stand as a united front as God has commanded.

Prayer

Lord, help to respectfully leave my parents as I focus on You and my husband in marriage. Give me a quiet and gentle spirit when establishing boundaries for my marriage. Father, help my husband to do the same. Let no one come between my husband and I as we seek to place You at the center of our union. Let no man come between what You have joined together. Lord, sometimes it is hard, feelings get hurt but give us strength and eyes to see as You see. We ask this in Your Holy Name. Amen.

Action Plan

If you haven't already established your family "rules" or values, sit down with your husband and agree on what priorities you have including how you will spend holidays, how you will handle interference with each other's family.

Discuss practical ways you can put your husband and marriage first.

Study Guide

Have you identified a relationship that may be interfering in your marriage? If so, which one(s)?

What boundaries can you establish to prevent this relationship from affecting your marriage?

We looked at placing children as idols. Do you see yourself in any of these signs?

What is God telling you about the relationships that come in contact with your marriage?

Are they honoring Him or degrading your marriage?

How would you rate your relationship with your mother in law?

How can YOU improve the relationship?

Do you complain about your husband to others, including your mother?

What is God telling you about this area?

What was new or stood out to you in this chapter?

In what ways were you challenged or encouraged?

After completing this chapter, how do you feel God is calling you to pray for your marriage?

Chapter 7

Sex & Intimacy

We have covered quite a bit and God (and us) still have some work to do. In this chapter, we will be discussing sex and intimacy in marriage.

I want to start by reading this passage from 1 Corinthians:

> 6 Now for the matters you wrote about: "It is good for a man not to have sexual relations with a woman." 2 But since sexual immorality is occurring, each man should have sexual relations with his own wife, and each woman with her own husband. 3 The husband should fulfill his marital duty to his wife, and likewise the wife to her husband. 4 The wife does not have authority over her own body but yields it to her husband. In the same way, the husband does not have authority over his own body but yields it to his wife. 5 Do not deprive each other except perhaps by mutual consent and for a time, so that you may devote yourselves to prayer. Then come together again so that Satan will not tempt you because of your lack of self-control.

Whew. Ok. Let's unpack this for a moment. This passage addresses being faithful, submitting our bodies our husbands and not withholding marital relations, except for prayer and fasting.

That's a lot of marital advice in just a few verses. We could spend weeks just on this one topic, but I want to address a few important matters.

1) Sex is a gift from God
2) Sex and intimacy are not the same
3) Using sex as a weapon

Marriage is full of challenges. God created us to be unique and bringing two unique individuals together in marriage can present a host of potential difficulties. From how we spend money and time to different personality styles and from child disciplining to taking out the trash, daily married life presents numerous opportunities for our uniqueness to clash. One of the most damaging potential clashes, however, is one that takes place in the bedroom.

As we are all unique, created that way by our Father who loves us, we bring differing levels of sexual desire to the marriage. You may have had a greater desire for sex before you had children and now you are exhausted from doing it all that all you want to do is sleep when your head hits the pillow. Or, perhaps you and your husband have always been on different pages when it comes to how often you have sex. It is perfectly normal for our desires to change over time and with the seasons of our life.

There are dozens, maybe hundreds of studies or polls on how frequently married couples have sex. On marriage.com, they share a few of those poll results:

Newsweek magazine found in its poll that married couples have sex about 68.5 times a year, or a little more than on an average. The magazine also found out that as compared to unmarried people, married couples have 6.9 times more sex per year.

According to a University of Chicago Study called "The Social Organization of Sexuality: Sexual Practices in the United States," about 32 percent of married couples have sex two or three times a week, 80 percent of married couples have sex a few times a month or more, and 47 percent say they have sex a few times a month.

In another study, this time by David Schnarch, PhD, who studied more than 20,000 couples, 26% of couples have sex once a week, more likely once or twice a month.

What is normal for your marriage may be abnormal for the other couples in your small group (or neighbors). The normal for your marriage, however, needs to be something that you and your husband are comfortable with. When one partner is feeling neglected or pressured, it puts strain on the marriage. When one is not in the mood for sex and one always seems to be, the marriage can suffer.

Sex is a gift from God that allows us to have physical and emotional intimacy with our spouse. It is a time to recharge our marital batteries, so to speak, and reconnect with our beloved. So what do you do when you are not in the mood for sex, but your husband is?

In one of the resources for this chapter, I share seven tips for when you just aren't in the mood, but the point I want to get across is that God, in His design for marriage, created us to submit to our husbands, including in the bedroom.

We are not to withhold sex when we want to get our way. Or, for that matter, offer sex to get what we want. Sadly, women do this. Even Christian women. You may even have done this, in the past, but I implore you to use sex and intimacy as a vehicle for closer connection with your husband, not as a tool for manipulation.

If you and your husband have different sex drives, and most of you will, I encourage you to talk about it and come to an agreement on what is comfortable for both of you.

There are some questions in the action plan for you to start this conversation. It may be uncomfortable. Many of us are raised not to discuss sex, but, as God created sex for marriage, this is a healthy conversation to have and one, that in the end, seeks to glorify Him in your marriage.

Sex

Sex is an important part of marriage. It was designed by God for many reasons including procreation, pleasure, stress relief and even physical or emotional release.

If you remove sex from marriage, you can run the risk of putting up barriers to intimacy. Of course, there are seasons when sex is not possible or practical (immediately following childbirth or surgery, illness, separation, to name a few) and there will be marriages where sex is not physically possible for health or other reasons. In those cases, the couple will need to look for other ways to increase intimacy. We'll address the difference between sex and intimacy in the next chapter.

Outside of the reasons listed above, sex is an important and healthy part of marriage. Let's look at several reasons that sex is beneficial in marriage (outside of procreation).

Sexual intimacy brings you closer together

Immediately after sex, couples feel a deep connection. One of love and closeness and intimacy. When couples go for a time without sex, they tend to feel a disconnect. Sex connects us to our spouses both physically and emotionally. It creates a bond with our husbands that we cannot have with any other human being.

Sexual intimacy allows you to become more selfless

Having satisfying sex is usually the result of putting your spouse's needs before your own. Considering your husband's needs, wants and desires (and him considering yours), is a selfless act and connects the two of you on a deeper level.

Occasionally, you won't have time for the sex that allows you to focus on the other's needs. Let's be frank here, sometimes a "quickie" is all that you can fit in. And, while there is a time and a place for that, sex where you focus on the other partner's needs, fills a void that both partners are lacking without it.

Sexual intimacy makes your husband feel loved

Of course, in most marriages, both spouses feel a deep connection after sex, but this is especially true for men. Many men, have a love language of physical touch (see chapter two for more on this). They often report feeling most loved after sex with their spouse. While this can be true for women, as well, men are, by God's design, more physical creatures.

Having Sex Helps to Put God at the Center of Your Marriage

I know, I know. You may think that this one is a stretch, but bear with me for a minute. God created sex for husband's and wives. He has pretty clear guidelines for it (see 1 Corinthians 7:1-5). It's clearly an important part of our marriage union and by enjoying sex, we are pleasing God and honoring Him.

The difference between sex and Intimacy

There are many types of intimacy but few types of sex. With sex, we have *sex* and *making love*. With intimacy, there are more varieties.

Types of intimacy include:

1) **Physical intimacy** – this includes sex, but also, holding hands, kissing, hugging, or cuddling up watching your favorite television show.
2) **Recreational intimacy** – this is the connection you form when you perform activities together (bowling, browsing a museum, catching or playing a baseball game).
3) **Emotional intimacy** – part of communication, this type of intimacy is formed or bolstered by sharing feelings, emotions, and discussing life experiences with each other.

4) **Intellectual intimacy** - connecting with each other through discussion. Discussion can be anything from the books you are reading to world news and politics, but lively discourse can strengthen the intimacy between a husband and wife. This is an extension of communication in chapter 4. This type of intimacy is critical to marital success.

5) **Spiritual intimacy** - being in the word together, praying together and for one another, and worshiping together

Often, spouses (men more so than women), confuse sex and intimacy. They also tend to be able to separate sex from intimacy than women. Women, on the other hand, usually relate sex to intimacy more closely.

What can you do to strengthen each of the five areas of intimacy? Dig into this, prayerfully, in the study guide of this chapter.

Infidelity (and recovering from)

Christian marriages are not immune from infidelity. In fact, according to Dr. Willard F. Harley Jr., a licensed psychologist in Minnesota and author of the best-selling book His Needs, Her Needs: Building an Affair-Proof Marriage, 60 % of married couples will experience infidelity at some point in their marriages. 60%!!!

Infidelity can take many forms. It is not necessarily sex with another. It can be an emotional affair. This type of cheating is much more common than the physical type and can be just as damaging. It starts innocently enough. Sharing a cup of coffee or lunch with a coworker or chatting with a friend online. The break comes when this conversation turns to matters that should only be discussed with your spouse. Such as problems in the marriage. When one spouse does not feel loved, appreciated or heard, they look for those feelings elsewhere.

Emotional cheating often turns into physical cheating.

There's another type of infidelity that we should also be aware of: object infidelity. This type of infidelity is when one spouse places and object (or a job, or hobby, even a phone) in front of his or her spouse. This type of cheating, similar to idol worship, is strictly forbidden in the Bible. Remember that God has ordained our priorities to be Him, our spouse and then everything else.

How do we protect ourselves and our spouses from infidelity? First, we keep God at the center of our marriage. We strive to please Him first. When you seek God in all you do, you don't want to disappoint Him.

Second, we avoid situations that can lead to infidelity. Recently, we invited a couple from church to have lunch with us. The husband offered his phone number for us to connect with him. My husband didn't have his phone on him and asked me to save this man's number in my phone. I was hesitant, but I did as asked, then, when we returned home, had my husband save the man's number and I deleted him from my phone. Why? I did not want to text a man other than my husband.

Avoid putting yourselves in situations that can cross a line. I never share a meal with or just meet for coffee, with any man other than my husband, unless my husband is present. It's not that I don't trust myself to be faithful. It's that I value my husband and my marriage over everything except God.

A text here and there can lead to deeper conversations which can lead to emotional and even physical cheating.

Discuss with your husband what your boundaries should be and stick to them.

If you or your husband work outside of the home, commit to not having lunch or being alone with the opposite sex.

Third, actively work to increase the intimacy in your marriage so that you have no need to look for it outside of your marriage union.

Fourth, avoid pornography or impure images and situations.

Finally, avoid secrets. Unless you are planning a surprise party for your spouse, don't keep secrets from each other. Secrets can turn into lies and lies can turn into deeper sin. Secrets put up a barrier to intimacy that grows higher and deeper and can be the catalyst for infidelity to occur.

If your marriage has been affected by infidelity

Without getting too deep into it, I will share that my late first husband was a serial cheater. He cheated both physically and emotionally and it wrecked me. If you are familiar with my story, then you know, my husband was not a believer. We tried counseling and I tried prayer, but in the end, he still left me for someone else.

Your story does not have to be like mine. Marriage **can** recover from infidelity.

It may take years of rebuilding trust, setting boundaries and strengthening intimacy, but it can be done. I would highly recommend a qualified Christian counselor to guide you through the painful process. Both the spouse that was unfaithful and the betrayed spouse will have wounds that need to heal. It took me years (and God is still not finished with me) to heal from those wounds. I still have a hard time letting people in emotionally and trusting others stemming from the years of infidelity that I endured.

I'm blessed to be married to a man now that loves the Lord and is faithful, but my emotional baggage has stayed with me for years.

My load is lightening and the wounds are fading, but they are not completely gone.

Prayer

Father God, please keep my husband and I sexually pure in mind and body. Help us to avoid anything lustful or immoral, keeping our marital bed a sanctuary.

God, we both have pasts, please help us heal from those pasts particularly where those pasts are encroaching on our marriage. Remind us both that we have been forgiven by you.

Lord, I pray that we will have eyes for no one else but each other. Take away any temptation and shield our eyes from anything unpure.

Help me to feel beautiful, the way that You made me. Help me to accept and appreciate the body that you have given me and my own sexuality. Please help my husband and I learn how to experience pleasure and intimacy in the marriage bed.

I recognize that an important part of marriage is sexual. Help me to never use sex to manipulate my husband or use it to get my way but withholding it or giving it.

Heavenly Father, You have created sex and intimacy as a gift for husband's and wives. Let us always view it that way and remember You in how we live our sexuality.

In Your Son's Holy Name. Amen.

Action Plan

Discuss the satisfaction of your sexual life with your spouse. Use these questions to get the conversation started. Let the conversation go from there:

Are you satisfied with the amount of sexual relations we have? What would be an ideal frequency? (Each of you may need to compromise here).

Is there something that you would like to try in the bedroom? (Please see the resources section for some helpful information regarding sexual activities Christian marriage bed).

What do I do in bed that you most enjoy?

What do I do in bed that you don't enjoy?

What can I do more of?

Study Guide

Are you satisfied with your sex life? Why or why not?

Ask God for words and wisdom and discuss your marital relations with your husband. Then come back and write a prayer to God for help in this area.

List the five areas of intimacy. What are three ideas you have to strengthen each of these areas in your marriage?

What is God telling you about the sex and intimacy in your marriage? What changes can you make to please your husband both sexually and intimately?

Use a concordance and look up several verses on sex in marriage. Then use these verses to pray over the sex and intimacy in your marriage.

How do you express affection for one another outside the bedroom? Are you both comfortable and happy with this aspect of your relationship?

What are your individual expectations with regard to sex in marriage? How do they compare with your spouse's? If you differ, how will you resolve the differences?

What, in your opinion, are the five most important factors in a marriage? How would you rank them? Where did you put sex in your rankings? Why did you rank them this way?

Chapter 8

Money & Finances

As we begin to wind down our study, we need to talk about the elephant in the room: Money. Money and differing opinions on how to manage it, has long been a top reason for divorce, even in Christian marriages. One spouse may be a spender, the other a saver. One may never balance a checkbook, the other balances it down to the penny and will spend hours tracking down purchases if the checkbook is off by just a few cents.

God gives us money through our vocations and other means, but it is up to us to be good stewards of that money. Are you and your spouse "on different pages" when it comes to money management?

How you handle money as a couple is important, not just for day to day avoidance of conflict, it is a way to honor God.

By being good stewards of the resources He has given you, you are praising and worshipping Him.

How is it the elephant in the room? Many couples avoid talking about money until there is a problem and often, that discussion leads to arguing.

In today's reading, we'll look at several ways to avoid financial conflicts all while honoring our Heavenly Father.

Here are some tips to prevent money from being a thorn in your marriage as well as how to honor God through the way you and your husband handle money:

1. As with any topic, pray about money. Pray that God will help you manage it in a way that is pleasing to Him.

2. No matter how tempting to keep separate accounts, have joint bank accounts. This encourages transparency and avoids secrets in how each of you spend your money. If you have separate bank accounts, how would you feel if your husband looked over your bank statements? If you have nothing to hide, you are on the right track. If you don't want your husband to see how much money you spent at the mall or the craft store, I recommend praying about this issue and asking God to reveal to you what needs to change. Is it by combing your bank accounts? Setting aside time each month to look over each other's statements? Perhaps, it is changing the way you spend money.

3. When money, including bank accounts, are separate, it encourages a "his and mine" mentality. This can be dangerous in a marriage and can provide the flint to spark fights in a marriage.

   "Seek first the kingdom of God and his righteousness, and all these things will be added to you." - Matthew 6:33

4. Talk with your spouse about money. Preferably before you get married, but even if you have been married for years, this is important. Discuss tithing, saving, priorities on what to spend money on. Decide who will pay the bills and what "checks and balances" you will put in place for accountability.

5. Keep good records of money. No matter which spouse manages the checkbook, both should know where to find important financial records and how to read them.

6. Together, increase your knowledge about money. Take a course, read a book about investing together, watch videos on how interest works.

7. Create a budget together. When you look at how the money in your house is being spent, you find opportunities to improve and plan for the future. It's recommended that you look over your budget at least once a month to make sure you are staying on track. If you find that you are spending more (or less) every month on certain areas of your budget, it's time to adjust the budget and look for additional ways to save.

8. Set guidelines for how to spend money. In my house, any purchase over $100 requires both spouses to agree. It may be more or less in your home, but if you set these standards in advance, you are less likely to have arguments later about how money is spent.

A note on tithing: If both spouses are Christians, they know that giving God the first tenth is commanded in the Bible. Tithing is God-ordained and our first priority should be pleasing Him. If you are married to an unbeliever, this area is a bit more tricky, but the wife is to submit to her husband in order to lead him to the Lord.

Wives, in the same way submit yourselves to your own husbands so that, if any of them do not believe the word, they may be won over without words by the behavior of their wives,

1 Peter 3:1-6

Prayer

Dear Lord, we trust in you and how you provide for us. You are Jehovah Jireh, the Lord who provides. We thank you for all that we have and for the blessings you have given us. We ask you to shield us from the doubts and fears we have with regard to money and finances.

Let us not make money and idol and help us to rest in the knowledge that You are enough. You have given the sparrows food and will meet our every need.

Please help us to be good stewards of our money, diligent in all spending, accountable in tithing to you, consistent in saving and willing to be generous to others in need. Bless us O Lord! Help us to be content with what we have as you give unto us. Please help us to place our trust in you and not ourselves.

Action Steps

Schedule a block of time to sit down with your husband to talk about money. Include guidelines for spending it, financial goals, setting a budget and division of financial responsibilities.

Use the printout in this chapter's resources to guide you on setting financial goals.

Study Guide

Are you honoring God in how you and your husband handle money? If not, what changes need to be made?

What does the Bible say about debt and credit?

What did Jesus mean when He said, It is easier for a camel to go through the eye of a needle than for a rich man to enter the kingdom of God?

What does the Bible tell us regarding our financial priorities?

What are we modeling to our children in the way we handle finances in our marriage?

Using a concordance, look up some verses in the Bible about money. Journal them and pray over them, asking God to shine a light on any area of your finances that does not honor Him.

Do you currently tithe? Why or why not? If not, pray over how God instructs us to tithe and to give you the words and wisdom to discuss tithing with your spouse.

Chapter 9

Friendship, Fellowship and Godly Mentors

Our time together is flying by (or is it just me?). We've covered everything from intimacy and money as well as family and forgiveness. Hopefully, you've learned some tools to keep Christ at the center of your marriage where it relates to these topics.

In this chapter, we are going to spend some time discussing friendship, fellowship and godly mentors.

You may have heard the saying "you are who you spend your time with". The Bible mentions friendships throughout including these verses, from Proverbs:

Proverbs 12:26 The righteous choose their friends carefully, but the way of the wicked leads them astray.

And

Proverbs 27:17 As iron sharpens iron, so a friend sharpens a friend.

On this chapters printable scripture cards, I've included ten of my favorite verses on friendship.

These verses illustrate that being a friend, according to the Bible, means laying down your life for your friend, encouraging and building one another up, "sharpening" another, lifting another up - even keeping each other warm!

So what does this have to do with marriage?

Friends, like family, can have a profound impact on a marriage. Well-meaning friends can give bad advice or even insert themselves into a marriage if both spouses aren't careful.

Surrounding yourself with friends that edify and respect boundaries can have the opposite effect and help the marriage to stay strong.

Consider the friends in your life. Would they lay down their life for you? Do you speak encouraging words and build you up? Do they support you and your marriage? Do you sharpen each other? For iron, or knives, you sharpen them by running two blades together - how does this relate to your friendships?

One of the best examples of true friendship is demonstrated in the friendship of David and Jonathan, son of Saul. According to Gotquestions When David was being hotly pursued by Saul, Jonathan sought David out "to help him find strength in God" (1 Samuel 23:16), which leads us onto our second point. Iron sharpening iron is an opportunity to fulfill the Law of Christ. The apostle Paul says that we are to carry and share the issues and burdens that we face daily, to lament over personal sin, advise on how best to repent of it, and rejoice over the conquest of it. This is the same "royal law" mentioned in James 2:8, where we are exhorted to love one another.

What a beautiful picture of friendship!

I would be remiss, though, if I didn't point out that TOO much carrying of each others burdens might place a strain on a marriage.

As mentioned in a previous chapter, be very careful what you share about your marriage to your friends. Talking about your husband negatively can cloud your friend's perception of your spouse. They may be more likely to give advice that is not biblical or just plain bad.

It may also be disrespectful to your spouse.

If you are having a disagreement with your husband, don't discuss it with your friend or neighbor. Talk to your husband about it.

While this verse in Matthew is directed toward dealing with conflict in the church, the lesson is applicable to marriage, as well:

Matthew 18:15

15 "If your brother or sister[a] sins,[b] go and point out their fault, just between the two of you. If they listen to you, you have won them over.

If the two of you are having an argument or he hurts your feelings, share it with him.

If you deem the offense unresolvable or your environment it is physically unsafe, seek a Christian counselor or your pastor to talk to.

When we are badmouthing our husband to others, not only is his reputation affected, but yours is, as well. It also pulls outsiders into private issues in your marriage.

In our reading today, we'll talk a bit more about good friendships, as well as fellowship with other believers and godly mentors.

Friendships

Friendships are an important part of life, especially the Christian life. As we know, iron sharpens iron. If we have friends who do not share our beliefs, pitfalls in our life and our marriage may occur.

Let's be real for a minute here. When you spend time with friends who are not followers of Christ, are you more or less like to engage in sinful behavior? Are you more or less likely to keep your focus on God? I think we know the answer here.

I'm not saying that you should only have Christian friends. I'm saying that you are you who spend time with. Your focus cannot be of this world and of God at the same time.

Of course, we are to be the light in the darkness and witness for Christ, but we have to choose when and where. You are more likely to make the right choices and have a closer walk with God if you surround yourself with other women who love Jesus.

If you have friends who like to party and who don't go to church – you are more likely to party and not go to church.

If you have friends who like to spend tons of money on clothes and shoes – you are more likely to make poor choices regarding your own spending habits.

No matter how old we are, we are still subject to succumbing to peer pressure. It doesn't mean we are bad people, it just means that when we are around those who make poor choices, we are more likely to make poor choices.

Let me give you an example. I have a friend we'll call Lisa. Lisa is divorced and is more into spiritual woo woo concepts than God. She likes to flirt with men and go to parties. She also has a tendency to drink – a lot. Now, I love her to pieces and enjoy spending time with her. We are both entrepreneurs and both from the east coast so we have lots in common to chat about, but I have to limit my time with her.

A trip to run errands will turn into stopping at the winery which leads to staying out too late and, on at least one occasion, has caused me to miss church in the morning.

Lisa isn't a bad person, but being around her makes it more likely that I will make choices that aren't right for me or my relationship with God.

While having non-Christian friends is fine, think before you say yes to their invitations to ensure that you continue to make the best choices for you and your walk with God.

I'm still working on finding some more Christian women friends in my area. I work from home and don't get out much, other than church and ministry activities, but I'll share with you the ideas that I have for surrounding yourself with other Christian women friends.

• Attend events hosted by the Women's Ministry at your church.

• Ask an acquaintance from church out for coffee

• Make friends with other women in online groups and Facebook pages – look for others in your area

• Attend a Bible study at a local church

• Assist in a ministry at church to get to know others

Think for a moment: are your friendships honoring God? Are they honoring your marriage? If you aren't sure, ask your husband what he thinks. At the very least, it will provide an opportunity to discuss heart mattes.

Your Husband's Friendships

Let's consider your husband's friendships. When thinking of your husband's circle of friends, would you say they are good, godly influences on him? Do these friendships build up and edify your husband? If you have any concerns, I encourage you to prayerfully, then lovingly, discuss your concerns with your husband.

Often, married men with single friends can struggle with this. The single friends have ample time to pursue hobbies, travel and just "hang out with the guys". When the single friend "ribs" his married friend about how they never hang out any more or tries to encourage them to spend more time with their friends, issues can arise.

The married man may feel guilt from his friends or start spending less time at home. Again, if this is an issue in your marriage, I encourage you to discuss it with your husband. If you can't resolve the issue, consider finding a Christian counselor that can give you wise counsel.

Friendships with the Opposite Sex

Can married men and women be friends with the opposite sex? Ooh boy. This one can be tricky. There are a few different scenarios or combinations we could look at here:

A single woman and a married man.

A married woman and a single man.

A married woman and a married man.

With any of these combinations, there are several factors to consider:

What do these or should these friendships look like? Should they even exist? Does God prohibit them as inappropriate, or can they be part of a healthy church community?

I don't think there is an easy answer here. For each friendship, or potential friendship, risks should be weighed. If you or your husband have a friendship with a member of the opposite sex, consider each of these risks and discuss, as a couple, if the friendship honors God and your marriage. If it does not, it may be necessary to put some distance between those friends.

1. Risk of poor boundaries
2. Risk of unreciprocated feelings
3. Risk of sexual or intimate temptation
4. Risk of undermining marriage

Risk of Poor Boundaries:

Every relationship, including marriage relationships, but certainly friendships need boundaries. Those boundaries will be unique to the parties in the relationship. So what are appropriate boundaries for a male and female friendship? They should include:

No private text messages (or Facebook messages)

No private or secret meetings or get-togethers (either include your spouse or another Christian friend or, at least receive the blessing from your spouse before meeting).

No detailed discussion of marriages, sex or other intimate relationship matters.

Risk of Unreciprocated Feelings:

Innocent intentions, friendships, may lead to love. After all, that is how many marriages occur. One person may have simply friendly intentions, but the other may begin to develop feelings. If that occurs, to honor God and your marriage, that friendship needs to come to an end.

Take care to hold fast to your boundaries to avoid friendships developing into deeper feelings and having the potential to betray.

Risk of Sexual or Intimate Temptation:

I don't believe that married people begin an opposite sex friendship with the intention to cheat. It is when we become intimate (including having intimate discussions) that the door can open, even slightly, to sexual attraction. Once that door is open, it can be difficult to close.

Intimacy can lead to sexual temptation. Discussing intimate matters with a person of the opposite sex allows for vulnerability and vulnerability may be the spark that turns into a glance, a wink or a coy smile and that can turn into infidelity.

Risk of Undermining the Marriage:

When friendship becomes more important (in word or action) than our marriage or when we share intimate details about our spouse or our marriage with a friend of the opposite sex, we are undermining a union that God had ordained.

Some signs that your friendship with the opposite sex are undermining your marriage:

Are we spending time alone together?

Are our meetings (especially locations) increasingly private?

Are we complaining about our marriages (or love life) to each other?

Are we texting each other privately?

Do I find myself thinking about them, or fantasizing about a life with them?

Do I find myself excusing intimacy that would be otherwise inappropriate?

Having friendships with the opposite sex is an area that needs to be regularly examined by both you and your husband to ensure that you are both maintaining boundaries that are both healthy for your marriage and pleasing to God.

Fellowship

Throughout this course, we have talked about surrounding yourself with other believers (family, friends, church) so I won't get too much into this here. I just want to point out that as mentioned "iron sharpens iron". Fellowship with other believers is incredibly important for you to grow as a believer and a wife.

At the beginning of the church in Acts 2, we see a glimpse of fellowship with other believers:

"They devoted themselves to the apostles' teaching and to the fellowship, to the breaking of bread and to prayer. Everyone was filled with awe, and many wonders and miraculous signs were done by the apostles. All the believers were together and had everything in common. Selling their poschapters and goods, they gave to anyone as he had need. Every day they continued to meet together in the temple courts. They broke bread in their homes and ate together with glad and sincere hearts, praising God and enjoying the favor of all the people. And the Lord added to their number daily those who were being saved." Acts 2 (NIV)

Ideally, Christians help other Christians to be accountable to God's teaching. They encourage one another and provide correction when we go off course.

If you find that you are lacking in fellowship with other believers, consider one of the following ways to enjoy fellowship:

- Join a small group
- Attend Bible study

- Volunteer in missions or ministires
- Invite a fellow congregant to lunch or coffee

What else would you add?

Godly Mentors

Having a mentor can be a powerful tool for your marriage. A mentor can provide personal instruction and allow you to share your fears, concerns and needs in a safe environment.

A mentor invests in your life and your marriage by teaching you, encouraging you and sometimes motivating you.

Mentoring is a biblical concept. In Titus 2, older men are encouraged to train the younger men and older women are told to train the younger women.

Titus 2:4-5

4 Then they can urge the younger women to love their husbands and children, 5 to be self-controlled and pure, to be busy at home, to be kind, and to be subject to their husbands, so that no one will malign the word of God.

Where do you find mentors? Mentors can be found almost everywhere. They may be in your neighborhood, your church or even your family. A mentor may be older or younger than you. What is important is not age, but character and biblical knowledge and living.

I encourage you to identify at least one woman mentor as well as a married couple who can mentor you and your husband in your marriage journey.

Spend time with your mentor (this can be formal, regular meetings or informal). Ask questions and ask them to teach you something that you desire to learn about life, marriage or homemaking.

Prayer

Dear Lord, I pray that you bless my husband and I with wholesome friends who love you like we do and thank you for the friends you have already placed in our lives.

Father, I ask that you reveal mentors to us who we can trust to guide us when the marriage waters get rough. We ask that you surround us with other believers so that we may form good, godly friendships to build each other up and keep each other accountable to Your Word and our marriage vows.

Lord, thank you for the gift of friendship with my husband and others. Your Word teaches us that when we walk with the wise we become wise; and when we associate with fools we get in trouble. Please help us to form and strengthen friendships with wise people.

In Your Son's Holy and precious Name. Amen.

Action Plan

Identify the friends in your life. Consider each friendship. Does it build you up? Does this friend support your marriage? Are there people that you should distance yourself from for the security of your marriage?

Ask your husband to make a similar list. Then discuss each of the friends. You may be surprised to find that you or your husband may not agree on which friends are healthy for your marriage.

Brainstorm potential godly mentors for each of you and for your marriage. When you agree, prayerfully consider asking that person(s) to act as your mentor.

If fellowship with other believers is lacking in your marriage, make a commitment to join a small group or attend the next event at your church.

Study Guide

What are the attributes of a good friend?

When you are looking for a friend, what quality is the most important to you?

Which quality of a friend from Proverbs do you tend to overlook?

Has that ever been harmful to you or your friendships?

In what one way do you think you could be a better friend?

Who are the godly friends in your life?

Are you a good friend, according to the Bible?

Do you have a godly mentor in your life or marriage?

If so, what role does this mentor have in your life?

If not, see this chapter's action plan and identify one or more.

Are you surrounding yourself with believers in fellowship?

If not, what is stopping you?

Use this chapter's Scripture cards and/or a concordance and find a few verses on friendship in the Bible. Journal them and pray that God blesses you with good, godly friends.

Why do you think having good, Christian friends pleases God?

What impact do your current friendships have on your marriage?

Are they positive or negative?

What changes do you need to make?

Wrap Up

Whew! We made it! During our time together, we've covered a lot of material. Are you feeling good about placing God at the center of your marriage?

Is Our Heavenly Father the first strand in your cord of three?

A God centered marriage is not a one-time deal. It is making daily choices to honor Him in your communication, your sexuality, your finances, your family, your friendship and every other detail of your life.

I encourage you, if you haven't already, to print out the reading material, study guides and other printables in this course. Keep them in a binder and revisit an area each week to remind you how to keep Him at the center of your marriage.

Marriage comes with challenges, but by seeking His face in the big and small details of your life and your marriage, we are more likely to overcome the challenges with our marriages intact.

Making God the center and highest priority of your marriage is the key to a healthy, thriving union with your spouse. If you are struggling in one area or another, take a good, prayerful look at that area and ask yourself: does God and His Word come first in this area? If not, take the steps to put Him first and watch the rest fall into place.

A God centered marriage means knowing Him, His Word and reflecting Him in our words and actions.

What do you need to do today to place Him at the head of your marriage? I'm praying for you, my friends!

ABOUT THE AUTHOR

Susan is a writer, speaker and the creator of Women of Noble Character ministries. She is passionate about helping Christian women live a Proverbs 31 life in today's world. The Lord laid upon her heart to serve women to grow in Christ, improve their marriages and manage their homes stress-free. She provides tools and resources on her website for Christian women to grow in their faith, deepen their relationship with their husbands and manage their homes well.

She lives in rural North Central Missouri with her handsome and hilarious husband and a myriad of dogs, cats and chickens.

Susan runs on Jesus, coffee and not enough sleep.

Made in the USA
Columbia, SC
23 June 2018